GAZA!

The Fallout From Premeditated Barbarianism

Ramon Bennett

SHEKINAH

Colorado Springs — Jerusalem

All quotations within the text proper are enclosed within quotation marks, quotations set off do not require quotation marks. All direct quotations from the Bible are indicated by italics and are enclosed within quotation marks except for quotations set off. All **bold emphasis** within Bible quotations is the author's own. Proper names and lesser-known foreign words are italicized.

Second printing January 2015

Published and Distributed in the **United States** by:
Shekinah Books LLC,
755 Engleby Drive, Colorado Springs, Colorado 80930, U.S.A.
Tel: (719) 645-7722. eMail: usa@shekinahbooks.com.
Website: http://www.ShekinahBooks.com.

Distributed in **Israel** by: Ramon Bennett,
P.O. Box 37111, Jerusalem 91370.
eMail: armofsalvation@mac.com.

Distributed in **New Zealand** by:
Michael Bahjejian,
210 Collingwood Street,
P.O. Box 1483 Hamilton.
Tel.: (07) 834-1128. eMail: michaelba@clear.net.nz.

Distributed in the **United Kingdom** by:
John and Yvonne Hellewell,
5 Greenhill Ave., Hellaby, Rotherham, South Yorkshire S66 8HE.
Tel.: (0170) 954-4198. eMail: Yvonne.Hellewell@tesco.net.

Distributed in **Canada** by:
Grand Beach Imports,
Box 310 Grand Marais, Manitoba ROE OTO.
Tel.: 1-855-755-6730. eMail: grandbeachimports@aol.com.

Shekinah Books LLC is a division of *Arm of Salvation Ministries* headquartered in Jerusalem, Israel. Further information can be obtained at: www.ShekinahBooks.com

He who keeps Israel neither slumbers nor sleeps
(Psalms 121:4).

To the Israeli soldiers—the warriors—that fought and gave up their lives defending their country in Operation Protective Edge. Israel salutes you.

Contents

Preamble

THIS SHORT VOLUME IS primarily taken from this writer's blog posts written before, during, and after Israel's 50-day Operation Protective Edge, which was a military action launched against Hamas's rocket fire from Gaza into Israeli civilian areas in July–August 2014. Extracts from a newsletter article, also written by this writer during the war, is interwoven within the blogs, together with news snippets publicized after the war that give clarity to that which was written during the time of open hostilities.

The blog posts were written in haste in order to keep up with events as they happened; in the main, original blog post headings and content have been retained; additional content has been interspersed that allows better understanding of the original; however, these insertions are dated, but do little to disrupt the chronological order of events.

As is the nature of running blogs dealing with the same subject, some repetition of facts are inevitable; for this the writer begs the reader's patience.

These pages represent an accurate record of what took place at the time it took place; what caused it to take place, and the inevitable consequences of it having taken place.

1

Rounding up Hamas

ON JUNE 12, 2014 around 10:30 at night, three Israeli teenagers, Gilad Sha'er, aged 16, Naftali Fraenkel, also aged 16, and Eyal Yifrach, aged 19 years, went missing from a hitchhiking station where they were trying to get rides home after finishing religious studies in their schools in the West Bank—biblical Judea and Samaria. One of the 16-year-olds tried to make an emergency phone call and whispered "I'm being kidnapped," but the police, who receive hundreds of prank calls thought it was just another practical joke. Apart from repeatedly asking where the caller was, they did nothing. Almost five hours later the father of one of the teenagers arrived at the police station. He reported his son as missing.

It was to be another three hours before the Israel Defense Forces (IDF) launched a massive 20,000-person search named Operation Brother's Keeper in an attempt to find the boys, but the terrorists had by then had a seven-hour start. The city of Hebron was hermetically sealed off by the IDF and soldiers went house to house searching for the teenagers; they checked every cellar, attic, shed, and even the caves in the area; some homes were searched two or three times. Two known Hamas operatives, who had spent time in Israeli prisons for terror related crimes against Israel, were the prime suspects and they were missing from their homes. They have yet to be apprehended at the time of writing this post.

Hundreds of Hamas operatives throughout the West Bank, including members of the Hamas government, were arrested and interrogated by the IDF as it searched for the boys. Numerous weapons caches were uncovered, including machine guns, hand guns, explosives, and hand grenades. The arrests were Israel's way of hitting back at Hamas which Prime Minister Netanyahu and IDF intelligence categorically blamed for being behind the kidnappings. Hamas is recognized as a terror organization by Israel, Egypt, America, and the EU. Israel claimed to have had "hard evidence" of Hamas's guilt, even to the extent of knowing which cell within Hamas carried out the abductions.

Some 54 Palestinians who had been freed in Israel's last prisoner swap in October 2011 were rearrested for having violated the terms of their release, which they had read and signed at the time of their release. The simple fact that 54 of the prisoners released into the West Bank had flouted the agreement under which they were released brought a flurry of bills before Israel's Knesset (Parliament) aimed at limiting the power of presidential pardons. If the bills pass into law, future releases would classify all released prisoners as only being out on parole; this the lawmakers want to anchor into Israel basic law that, while lacking a constitution, has the same power. Other bills coming before the Knesset will limit prisoner swaps to a one-for-one basis rather than the ridiculous lop-sided swaps Israel has made in the past.

Israel's last prisoner swap in October 2011 released 1,027 Palestinian terrorists for a lone Israeli soldier, Gilad Schalit, whom Hamas had held in solitary confinement, refusing him Red Cross visits or any contact with the outside world for five years and four months. Swapping Palestinian terrorists for kidnapped Israelis only spurred more kidnapping attempts and Israeli security forces have had to work overtime in order to foil them.

Following the lop-sided Schalit deal, two wealthy Saudi businessmen independently made open-ended offers of one million dollars to anyone who can kidnap an Israeli for use as a bargaining chip for releasing Palestinian terrorists from Israeli jails. Such incentives helped spawn hundreds of kidnapping attempts against Israelis.

Hamas denied it had anything to do with the abduction of the three teenagers, but said it applauded those who carried it out. Hamas extracted more than a thousand prisoners from Israel in the Schalit deal and it has made no secret of the fact that it intends to kidnap more Israelis in order to facilitate similar deals. This, then, was the underlying motive for abducting the innocent teens. Hamas even produced posters showing a look-alike Israeli in IDF uniform, claiming the kidnapped boys were all soldiers, thus legitimizing their abduction. Throughout the Palestinian street a three-finger salute signifying three Schalits became the mode; it was everywhere, on posters, on hoardings, even on Palestinian television. An Arab member of Israel's Knesset, Haneen Zoabi of the Balad party, raised Israeli hackles when she said that the Hamas kidnappers were not terrorists, that they are forced "to resort to these measures until Israel sobers up a bit." And when two other Arab members of the Knesset, Afu Agbaria of the Hadash party and Balad Chairman Jamal Zahalka, also went on record arguing that Hamas was neither a terror organization nor was the Palestinian struggle terrorism, that it was "just a struggle to right an historical wrong," the Israeli public showed little patience and called for all three Arab members of Knesset to be removed from their posts. Israeli police recommended that criminal investigations be opened against them.

2

Arab barbarianism

FEAR FOR THE THREE boys' safety grew with each passing day; thousands of searches made throughout the West Bank brought no trace of the teenagers. Finally, a small group of searchers, some of which had élite tracker training, began to think like kidnappers and looked for signs that would normally be overlooked. On June 30 they found Naftali Fraenkel's eyeglasses in long grass and kept looking for overturned rocks and the like, anything that would indicate the abnormal. Eventually they found a decomposing body that was partly buried under rocks. They called for help and soon after IDF soldiers found the other two bodies in a hastily-dug grave and partially covered with rocks. Israeli politicians across the board said that the murderers were nothing less than animals.

The flag-draped bodies of the three teenagers were brought back to Israel and around 50,000 Israelis turned out for the burial. The boys' bodies were laid to rest side by side, next to those of the Maccabees. Then the truth began to come out.

The boy's recorded emergency telephone call was released for public broadcast. Listeners could hear the whispered "I've been kidnapped," which was shortly followed by muffled gunshots and a moan from one of the teenagers as he died. The telephone call, which had been a cry for help, quickly became the cause of death. The terrorists had heard the call and one shouted, "Get the phone!" and then ordered one of the boys to "put your head down." The terrorists thought the Israeli security forces were now after them so they shot the boys ten times then and there in the backseat of the car using a gun with a silencer. The recording continued with whooping, hollering, and singing in Arabic, interspersed with "Three! Three!," which was an allusion to the Hamas kidnapping of Corporal Gilad Schalit in June 2006, and for whom, years later,

Israel was forced to pay heavily for his release through a very lop-sided prisoner release.

It seems apparent to this writer that due to the frightened telephone call from one of the Israeli boys, along with the ten obviously muffled gunshots, Israeli intelligence must have been aware that the boys were dead, but everyone else was living in hope. However, an incensed Israeli leadership used the opportunity to gravely weaken Hamas in the West Bank by operating a dragnet, capturing every Hamas leader and operative found while searching for the boys or their bodies.

The morning following the abduction Israeli security forces found a burnt out car not far from the hitchhiking station. After examination of the vehicle's remains a number of bullet casings were found inside. The boys' bodies were found some 12 kilometers (7.5 miles) from the hitchhiking station in an open area on the outskirts of Hebron. If getting rid of the bodies were the purpose, it would have made more sense for the terrorists to burn them along with the car rather than putting them in a different vehicle, then carrying them across open ground before semi-burying them. Apparently, the objective was to swap the boys remains for live prisoners as was the case with Hizb'allah in July 2008. At that time Israel swapped five Lebanese prisoners, including the fiendish murderer Samir Qantar, for two black caskets containing the remains of two Israeli soldiers who had been abducted and taken to Lebanon following a Hizb'allah cross-border raid.

In April 1979, Samir Qantar, then aged 16, led four other Lebanese terrorists in the murder of an Israeli policeman and an Israeli family in Nahariya. After shooting the policeman, Samir and one accomplice broke into an apartment building and kidnapped a young father and his four-year-old daughter. The mother hid herself and a two-year-old daughter in a cupboard; however, in trying to prevent the toddler from crying and giving away the hiding place the mother accidentally suffocated her little daughter, greatly adding to her own trauma.

The father and the four-year-old daughter were taken to a nearby beach where the terrorists had left their rubber boat in which they had come the ten kilometers (6.2 miles) from Lebanon. The boat had been disabled so Samir shot the father in the back and then drowned him to ensure that he died. He then killed the four-year-old girl by smashing her head with rocks before finally crushing her skull completely with the butt of his rifle. Samir is lauded as a hero in Lebanon.

Although it had been assumed at the time of the abduction that the two Israeli soldiers were dead, the two caskets were the first confirmation that the two soldiers, captured by Hizb'allah had died. Presumably, the Hamas terrorists from Hebron were trying to emulate Hizb'allah's horrible action.

3

Rockets keep falling on my head

DUE TO THE **IDF** turning over virtually every stone in the West Bank and arresting Hamas operatives and ministers, rockets began to periodically fall on Israel's southern cities and towns, forcing residents to continually run for shelters. Southern Israeli residents were ordered by the Home Front Command to remain within 15 seconds of a bomb shelter. The international community makes much of the fact that Israeli fatalities from terrorist missiles are low when compared to Palestinian casualties from Israeli reprisal raids; however, it always fails to note that Israel has spent billions on building bomb shelters to protect its citizens while Hamas has not built any shelters in Gaza, apart from the fortified bunkers that Hamas leaders hide themselves away in and from where they are able to remotely operate missile fire. Hamas stores its munitions under and inside residential apartment buildings; thus they use Palestinian civilians as human shields, which raises the casualty rate from Israeli air-strikes.

As it also did during Operation Cast Lead from 27 December 2008 to 18 January 2009, Hamas embedded itself in schools and hospitals, thereby using even the most vulnerable members of the population as human shields. On July 10 Hamas spokesperson Sami Abu Zuhri told the terrorist group's television station that "the tactic of using Gaza residents as human shields is praiseworthy and effective against Israel." He added, "This policy reflects the character of our brave, courageous people."

When recent rocket salvos began to rain down upon Israel's southernmost cites and towns, the Israel Air Force (IAF) began making the inevitable retaliatory strikes at Hamas's munition factories and missile caches. Things went from bad to worse and soon Hamas was firing a hundred plus Qassam, Grad, Katyusha, and Syrian and Iranian-made rockets into Israel every day; sustaining barrages of one missile every minute.

Hamas began upping the ante and targeted larger, inland Israeli cities with longer range missiles that had more powerful warheads, which brought an even heavier response from the IAF. However, Hamas was betting on Israel not wanting a repeat of the 2008 Operation Cast Lead in which the IDF made a ground invasion of Gaza after the IAF had wreaked havoc on it from the air. Hamas was correct in reading Israeli reticence to launch another all-out-war in Gaza and Hamas continued to fire rockets ad infinitum and garnered valuable Arab recognition as being the defender of the Palestinians; this even at the risk of the IAF leveling more of Gaza's buildings which had escaped earlier skirmishes with Israel.

Unemployment in the Strip was running at more than 44 percent and virtually the only thing Gaza then produced was rockets. Factories for manufacturing them had sprung up throughout the Strip and those production centers were churning out thousands of missiles. On September 13, 2014, Hamas head, Khaled Mashaal, admitted that "Tens of thousands of our children and our people are engaged in manufacturing weapons and digging tunnels." It was those production centers, weapons storage areas, and tunnels that the IAF targeted.

Israel monitors Gaza's new and improved rocket versions as they are tested by being fired into the Mediterranean Sea. IDF intelligence says 70 percent of all Israeli civilians are within range of Gaza's missiles.

Israel mobilized 40,000 reserve soldiers and sent them to the Gaza border to await further orders. If Israel was going to launch a ground invasion of Gaza in order to hit Hamas heavily and bring quiet to Israel's Home Front, then the entire Israeli population had to be prepared to run to the bomb shelters.

For several years an Israeli law has been in force that requires every new house, apartment building, and factory being built to have a hermetically sealable bomb shelter for its residents and workers. Plus every city and town has public bomb shelters which officials open up when wars break out. And in the most southern towns, which bear the brunt of Hamas and other terror group's missiles, there are even portable rocket-proof shelters that are moved according to need, and fortified bus stops are built that double-up as bomb shelters. This has been the reason why there are so few Israeli casualties resulting from missile attacks from Hamas and other terrorist groups in Gaza or from Hizb'allah's rockets fired from Lebanon.

Over 10,000 rockets had fallen on Israel's southern towns since Israel forcibly uprooted its Gaza communities in 2005. Withdrawing from the area Israel had occupied for some 47 years quickly turned it into a terrorist haven and brought the terrorist threat even closer. However, the international community still takes every opportunity to berate Israel for not responding proportionately to the rockets. This writer has said elsewhere, but will say it again, Israel should indeed respond proportionately: one rocket for one rocket. One rocket to be fired at a Gaza civilian population center for every rocket that is fired at an Israeli population center; there would be no need for Israeli air-strikes. A little taste of their own medicine would do the Palestinians a world of good and would most likely bring an end to the years-long rocket bombardment of Israel. As things stand today, in order to avoid as many civilian casualties as possible, the IAF usually waits until very late at night before hitting Hamas military targets in response to rocket attacks. The IDF will actually telephone civilians beforehand, warning them of imminent death if they do not vacate the buildings that are about to be bombed. Often the IAF drops a non-explosive bomb on top of the building—this is known as "a knock on the roof"—signaling that in around one minute's time a real bomb will hit the building and destroy it. Israel bends over backwards in its endeavor to keep Palestinian casualties to the minimum, but Hamas and other terror groups aim to cause as many Israeli civilian casualties as possible.

4

Jewish barbarity

UPON THE JUNE 30 news of the murder of the three Israeli teenagers a few unruly rightwing demonstrations in Israel calling for revenge took place. Israeli police arrested a number of the protesters who had gotten into violent scuffles with them. Several Israeli Facebook postings containing incitement against Arabs were put on the internet, one of which showed IDF soldiers in uniform calling for revenge against Arabs. Seven IDF soldiers associated with the page were arrested and placed in detention.

However, just two days after the bodies of the three Israeli teenagers were brought to Jerusalem for burial, a 16-year-old Palestinian boy, Muhammed Abu Khdeir, was abducted outside of his home around 4:00 a.m. as he prepared to go to the mosque for morning prayers. The abduction was recorded on CCTV, which the boy's father had installed on a building adjacent to his home, and he called the police. It only took an hour for the police to track down the Palestinian teenager due to his telephone pinpointing his location; however, when the police traced him to the Jerusalem forest the boy was found dead, murdered in the most monstrous fashion. In addition to a heavy blow to his head his body was burned. An autopsy showed inflammable material in his lungs, which clearly indicated that he had actually been burned alive.

Prime Minister Binyamin Netanyahu called the boy's parents to express his heartfelt condolences for the "despicable" and "heinous" crime committed against the boy. Israeli politicians from across the board condemned the atrocious crime in no uncertain terms. The mother of one of the murdered Israeli teenagers telephoned the Khdeir family, empathizing and sending her family's condolences.

Netanyahu ordered a fast-tracking of the murder investigation and within days several suspects were arrested and interrogated in connection with the Arab teen's murder. Israeli police said the killing of Abu Khdeir was the worst case of murder in Israel's modern history. Police said the investigation led them to believe the murder was most likely carried out as a revenge attack for the killing of the three Israeli teenagers earlier in June.

On July17 three suspects remaining in custody were indicted for Abu Khdeir's murder; two are 17-years of age and the other aged 29. Their names were not immediately released due to laws regarding minors and for fear of revenge attacks. The three suspects have since confessed to the killing and reenacted the crime for the police. Details of the murder suspects were sketchy for some time because a gag-order had been placed on the investigation due to the age of two of the suspects, and also due to the extremely volatile situation in Israeli Arab areas, which had erupted into violence following the abduction of the Arab teen and which is ongoing at this time of writing five weeks later. However, the name of the elder suspect, 29-year-old Yosef Haim Ben-David, has been released and is he is expected to plead insanity due to having spent some time in mental institutions.

Let it be unequivocally said here that terrorism is terrorism, whether the terrorists are minors or adults, whether they are Muslims or Jews. The Hamas terrorists who murdered the three Israeli teenagers were called animals; the Jews who murdered the Arab teenager are no less animals than the Hamas animals. What awaits Hamas terrorist murderers must also await Jewish terrorist murderers. Palestinian murderers of Israelis often have their family homes destroyed as a deterrent against other would-be murderers of Israelis. The Israeli Jews that took part in Abu Khdeir's loathsome murder should also have their family homes destroyed. A nation cannot have one law for Arabs and another for Jews. Sauce for the gander is also sauce for the goose.

5

War on the streets

As was mentioned in part 3, violent Palestinian rioting broke out in Jerusalem and other parts of Israel following the abduction of the Arab teenager, Abu Khdeir. The riots increased in violence upon the discovery of his body and rose to new heights after publication of the results of the autopsy detailing the teen's manner of death. Hundreds of Israeli Arabs took part in the riots, throwing rocks, molotov cocktails, fireworks, and pipe bombs.

Palestinian President Abu Mazen (Mahmoud Abbas) did uncharacteristically condemn the murder of the Israeli teens, but he then called upon the United Nations to rein in Jewish extremism following Abu Khdeir' murder. And this coming from a man who renames streets and squares after Palestinian murderers of Israelis, whether the murdered be men, women, or children. Abu Mazen designates six percent of the entire Palestinian economy for salaries being paid to imprisoned murderers of Israelis. Palestinian terrorists receive sentences proportionate to the amount of Israeli blood that he or she has shed. The more Israelis murdered the longer the sentence a terrorist receives; Israel does not utilize a death penalty. The longer the sentence the larger the monthly salary paid to the murderer; roughly four times the amount that which is paid to a Palestinian Authority (PA) public servant. Upon the murderers eventual release, often as a result of a prisoner swap, the released terrorists are hugged and kissed personally by Abu Mazen, who then hands them large cash sums—around $25,000—so they can build a new life. Sixty-eight percent of released terrorists return to terrorism; their years in prison apparently teaches them nothing; hatred of Jews fill their hearts and minds 24/7.

There were no disturbances among Arabs with Israeli citizenship over the odious murders of the three Israeli teens, but when the Arab teen, Abu Khdeir, was murdered, many hundreds of Israeli Arabs vented their rage at Israel. Israeli Arabs have the best conditions anywhere among the populations of the Arab world's 22 countries; only the few élite groups consisting of oil-wealthy Arab sheiks have it better. Israeli Arabs receive healthcare, child allowance, welfare, etc., but even so they still account for over 60 percent of all crime within Israel. Obviously, many of these Israeli citizens have no compunction about biting the hand that feeds them.

There are many fine, hardworking Israeli Arabs, but unfortunately they are greatly outnumbered by their kith and kin who continually take advantage of the system and never give anything back to their adopted country except trouble.

On July 6, in the midst of the days-long rioting, Prime Minister Binyamin Netanyahu said:

> Israeli Arab rioters cannot on the one hand throw petrol bombs and rocks, destroy property and call for the destruction of the state, and on the other hand enjoy the benefits of child allowance and National Security Insurance payments.

Several hundred Israeli Arabs were arrested by Israeli police during the violent confrontations and these may well have jeopardized their state benefits.

Despite Palestinian eagerness to live within Israel's borders, primarily in order to receive state benefits, which no other Arab population in the world enjoys, a multitude of those to whom Israel has granted citizenship and equal rights—approximately 1.2 million at this time of writing—cheer and celebrate whenever missiles and rockets are launched at Israel. It matters not whether the death raining from the skies came from Iraq during the reign of the late Saddam Hussein, or from Hamas and Islamic Jihad in Gaza and Hizb'allah in Lebanon, or whether it comes from the jihadists now fighting against Bashar Assad in Syria, or from any one of a hundred other Jew and Israel-hating Islamic groups. Many Israeli Arabs openly admit that they want to see Israelis suffer and die; hundreds will hand out candies, dance in the streets and on their rooftops when disaster strikes Israelis. Readers would be well advised to see Chapter 2 of this writer's book *Philistine: The Great Deception* for an in-depth, documented exposé of *The Arab Mind* and how it works.

In an appropriately timed September 21, 2014, article—which came to hand at the very moment of editing, extracts from which this writer has chosen to include—the PA's official daily newspaper *Al-Hayat Al-Jadida* claimed in headlines that Palestinians are better off working for Israelis.

After investigating working conditions for a group of Palestinians in the West Bank, employed by other Palestinians, the PA daily found that salaries and benefits were far higher right across the board for Palestinians working for Israelis in settlements.

The *Al-Hayat Al-Jadida* article, translated by Palestinian Media Watch, said that:

> whenever Palestinian workers have the opportunity to work for Israeli employers, they are quick to quit their jobs with their Palestinian employers—for reasons having to do with salaries and other rights.

The article praised conditions for Palestinians working for Israelis in West Bank settlements, while decrying the low salaries and lack of benefits for those workers employed by Palestinians. *Al-Hayat Al-Jadida* interviewed a number of Palestinian workers for the article, and found that those with Israeli bosses earned much more than those working for Palestinians—fully two times as much, plus paid sick leave, healthcare, vacation time, and free travel to and from work. Another plus for the Palestinians working for Israelis the article mentioned was that the Palestinian employees said that, unlike Palestinian employers, "Israeli employers can be relied upon to pay salaries."

There we have it from the horses mouth: Palestinian Arabs prefer to work for Israelis rather than their own people who merely exploit them. Israelis are not quite the ogres they are made out to be by the foreign media.

6

Death from the skies

FOLLOWING THE MURDER OF 16-year-old Abu Khdeir the Israeli Arab riots within Israel spiked and the periodic firings of missiles—rockets and mortar shells—moved into becoming constant 24/7 barrages. Rocket salvos increased and at night the IAF would retaliate firmly by targeting Hamas and Islamic Jihad terror cells preparing to launch rockets into Israel, together with striking underground rocket launchers and Hamas's weapons manufacturing plants.

Hamas had fallen upon hard times following the ousting of the Egyptian Muslim Brotherhood's Mohammad Morsi from the presidency by the Egyptian military. Hamas is an offshoot of Egypt's Muslim Brotherhood, and Hamas operatives were found to have broken Morsi, a former leader of the Muslim Brotherhood, out of prison during the riots that led to President Hosni Mubarak's overthrow. Hamas was also operating in Egypt's Sinai Peninsula against both Israel and the Egyptian military. It was involved in launching rockets into Israel and also helping Bedouin terrorists conduct ambushes against Egyptian security forces, which killed scores of Egyptian police and soldiers.

Egypt's military chief, Abdel Fatah al-Sisi, who was actually promoted to the position by Mohammad Morsi, led the Egyptian armed forces in a crackdown on the Muslim Brotherhood due to massive Muslim Brotherhood protests that led to hundreds being killed. Al-Sisi ousted Morsi from the presidency, placed him in detention and charged him, among a number of other things, with being a traitor. Al-Sisi was perceived by the Egyptian street as a hero. Riding a wave of popularity al-Sisi ran in the May 2014 presidential elections and was elected to the presidency in a landslide vote that garnered him 91.6 percent of the 26 million votes cast.

Al-Sisi virtually declared war upon Hamas and the Egyptian military have closed or destroyed in excess of 1,500 smuggling tunnels dug by Hamas under the Egyptian-Gaza border. The closure of the tunnels effectively severed Hamas's economic umbilical cord. It could no longer extract quantitative taxes from the dwindling number of smugglers bringing in fuel, gas, explosives, weapons, vehicles, and people.

Facing total collapse and unable to pay its government workers, Hamas decided to join with Abu Mazen's Fatah faction and form a unity government in a desperate act for survival. Almost the entire world hailed the PA-Hamas unity deal and within hours signaled that it was ready to work with the new unity government. Israel, however, had made it abundantly clear for months that under no circumstances would it ever negotiate or work with a government that included Hamas. After the signing of the unity agreement the Israeli leadership requested it be scrapped. Israel, they said, was prepared to continue negotiations with Abu Mazen's Palestinian Authority, but it would not work with a government that included Hamas, a terror organization committed to the destruction of Israel.

Abu Mazen guaranteed the new unity government had renounced terror, recognizes Israel, and would honor all past agreements signed with Israel. Hamas, on the other hand, said that Abu Mazen could not speak for Hamas, that Hamas would never recognize Israel, and that armed struggle was the only way to liquidate the "Zionist entity" that was occupying Palestinian land.

Rocket fire was ramped up against Israeli civilians and IAF responses grew heavier with each barrage. Major Israeli cities were targeted by Hamas missiles and each day Israelis were scrambling to find refuge in bomb shelters from the rockets. The more missiles launched against Israel's civilian population centers brought heavier and heavier responses from Israel. At the time of writing Hamas and its cadres had fired over 4,000 missiles into Israeli cities and towns and the IAF had dropped more than 2,000 tons of bombs, striking over 2,650 terrorist targets. Unfortunately, many Gazan civilians have been killed due to Hamas using them as human shields; Hamas is therefore responsible for their deaths.

Hamas is guilty of double war crimes: intentionally targeting Israeli civilians and using Gazans as human shields. It is not as if Hamas is ignorant of its crimes. On July 9, during an interview on Palestinian television, which was a discussion on whether

Palestinians should ask to join the International Criminal Court (ICC), the Ambassador to the United Nations Human Rights Council, Ibrahim Kraishi, said Palestinians had a weak case insofar as international law was concerned. Kraishi said:

> The indiscriminate launching of missiles against Israel constitutes a crime against humanity; every missile constitutes a crime against humanity, whether it hits or misses, because it is directed at civilian targets.

Kraishi said that by contrast Israel's actions follow legal procedures because the IDF warns Gazan civilians to leave sites before they are bombed. Hamas's leadership, however, implores Gazans not to leave their homes and encourages them to stand on roof tops. Hamas knows that Israeli warplanes will not strike a target if the pilot sees civilians in the target area.

7

Israel's ceasefires with itself

WITH THE ONGOING, EVER increasing rocket fire emanating from Gaza, many Israelis had been calling for the IDF to invade the Gaza Strip with ground forces in order to pummel Hamas *et al* into the ground once and for all. Hamas stores it arsenals under and in civilian apartment buildings, United Nations Relief and Works Agency (UNRWA) schools, and under public hospitals, even under Gaza's Shiva hospital, the main hospital in the Gaza Strip. Israeli intelligence knows where many of these weapons storage areas are, but to hit them with missiles from the air would cause catastrophic damage and the cost in human life would simply be too high. A prolonged ground invasion would be the only way to root out and destroy Hamas's multiple weapons' caches, but a prolonged ground assault would be fraught with danger for Israeli troops and cost many lives among Israel's finest young men. A ground invasion is always a last resort action and would only be undertaken should rockets continue to rain down upon Israel's population centers despite the aerial blitz.

Egyptian mediation efforts to get Israel and Hamas to agree to a ceasefire appeared to have a chance when on July 14, the eighth day of the war, an agreement was presented to the warring parties.

Israeli leaders, much to the chagrin of most of the population, accepted the ceasefire and halted Israel's air, sea, and artillery bombardment of Hamas targets at 9:00 a.m. on July 15. Hamas, however, dismissed the ceasefire overture and continued firing scores of rockets into Israel. An Israeli man, who was volunteering to distribute food to IDF soldiers on the border with Gaza, sustained severe wounds from a mortar barrage from Gaza during the "ceasefire" and quickly succumbed to his wounds. He was Israel's first direct casualty from Hamas's missile bombardments.

Israel continued to hold its fire even though there was no reciprocity from Hamas. Its rocket fire was even increased. Come first light the next morning Israel once again unleashed its firepower from the air and from the sea, and tanks positioned at Israel's southern border were given the coordinates for numbers of Hamas targets and they, too, joined the fray.

The United Nations pushed for a five-hour humanitarian truce that was to go into effect at 10:00 a.m. on July 17 in order to allow Gazans to stock up on food and medicines. The ceasefire went int effect; however, Hamas violated it by firing three salvos of rockets and mortars into Israeli towns during the "humanitarian" ceasefire. It became very apparent that Israel was observing ceasefires only with itself. Apparently, there are no humanitarian cells living in anyone that makes up the Hamas leadership.

A few of the leaders of Hamas live overseas in Qatari and Turkish four and five-star hotels, enjoying the opulence that wealth provides. Most of the local senior Hamas member live in luxurious homes with swimming pools, which are dotted throughout the Gaza Strip. Israel began targeting these homes, which double as command centers. Unfortunately, some, or occasionally all, family members often die alongside their men and fathers.

8

Facing Israel's firepower offensive and missile defense

WHEN HAMAS TREATED THE Egyptian ceasefire proposal with contempt and amped up its barrages of missiles into Israeli population centers, Prime Minister Netanyahu said Hamas's rejection of the ceasefire gave Israel justification to expand the military campaign against Gaza. Israel's security cabinet had accepted the ceasefire proposal and the IDF had held its fire in order for the truce to hold. Hamas was having none of it. Hamas ramped up its aggression against Israeli cities and towns, saying that it was not held by the Israeli decision to accept the Egyptian proposal. A problem for Hamas is that in rejecting the Egyptian proposal it has found itself unprecedentedly isolated in the Arab world. Egypt also accused Hamas of torpedoing the opportunity for calm and for giving Israel the legitimacy to mount a ground offensive into Gaza.

Israel's security cabinet echoed Netanyahu's earlier words and said, in response to Hamas's continuing rocket and mortar fire during the period of the "ceasefire," that Israel had broad international legitimacy to respond forcefully against Hamas. Conditions for Israeli residents of the southern towns had been untenable for years. They had never gotten used to having to remain within 15 seconds of a public bomb shelter or a private "safe" room. Children living under sporadic rocket fire since the day they were born are all but traumatized and many children have bed-wetting issues years after they should have grown out of it.

No people should be expected to endue such a hellish life as the residents of southern Israel have done. The southern Israeli towns and cities have had to endure over 14,500 rockets and mortars launched at them from Gaza with the express purpose of killing as many Israelis as possible.

In August 2005 Israel uprooted some 9,000 of its people that were living in Gaza communities and completely withdrew from the area. The international community had urged Israel for years to vacate Gaza, assuring Israel that in so doing there would finally be peaceful coexistence with the Palestinians. Israel left the area with intact greenhouses and flourishing agricultural businesses worth millions of dollars, believing it would help the Palestinian economy; however, the Palestinians looted and destroyed everything Israel left behind, including several synagogues which Israel foolishly believed the Arabs would revere. Hamas, Islamic Jihad, and other terror groups fought over the vacated land and built Hamastan, from where rocket fire has greatly intensified against Israel's southern towns and cities.

Due to the unending sporadic firing of rockets from Gaza into Israel the Israeli government pursued the development of the Iron Dome anti-missile defense system. It is an all-weather mobile air defense system designed to intercept rockets, mortars, and artillery shells from distances of four kilometers (2.5 miles) to 70 kilometers (43 miles) away. The Iron Dome's sophisticated radar determines the projectile's trajectory and if it will take it to a populated area it launches an interceptor missile, which has electro-optic sensors and steering fins that give it high maneuverability. The first Iron Dome saw active service in April 2011 when it successfully intercepted a Grad rocket fired from Gaza that was aimed at Beersheva.

Since April 2011 the Iron Dome has been continually upgraded in accuracy and distance; currently there are eight batteries in service, which are individually racking up 90 percent success rates. Each interceptor missile costs $100,000 and sometimes two interceptors are launched to ensure a positive hit on the incoming missile. The Iron Dome does not attempt to intercept every incoming projectile; if the system determines the projectile is heading for an open area it allows it to continue, fall, and explode.

Code-Red sirens are automatically activated by incoming missiles and Israelis dash for cover whenever a siren is heard. During Hamas's recent launching of hundreds of rockets into Israel every day, both short-range and long-range, the Iron Dome has intercepted hundreds over cities and towns, which not only minimizes damage to Israeli homes and buildings, but also frustrates Hamas *et al* whose sole intention is to destroy Israeli homes together with their occupants. There have been a number of injuries due to falling shrapnel following an Iron Dome intercept; Hamas's rockets are also packed with metal pieces that resemble ball-bearings and are designed to maximize casualties.

With no respite from rocket barrages the IDF intensified its aerial, artillery, and naval bombardments. It was limited in its effectiveness by Hamas ordering civilians not to flee their homes, many of which house Hamas munitions. However, the IAF wreaked havoc in Gaza by striking hundreds of terror targets, including several large weapons caches from the air. The Israel Navy had also done the same from the sea. The IDF foiled two Hamas terror attacks from the sea, killing all the terrorists, and also prevented several land attacks where terrorists had attempted to infiltrate an Israeli town, moshav, or kibbutz to murder or kidnap residents. Two large Iranian-made drones launched from Gaza were destroyed by Patriot missiles, and a planned terror attack, which would have used a number of hang gliders, was thwarted before it became actual due to Israeli intelligence learning of it. The leader of the hang gliding group, who was trained for the attack in Malaysia, was captured by Israeli security forces.

Around 80 percent of Gaza lost its electricity during the war. This, however, was not due to Israel cutting off the supply for non-payment of its multi-million dollar bill—which it would have the right to do—but was entirely due to Hamas rockets repeatedly being aimed at and hitting the Ashkelon power plant, blowing up the cables that carry Israel's electricity into Gaza. The Israel Electric Company received orders from National Infrastructure, Energy and Water Minister Silvan Shalom to avoid endangering its employees by fixing the downed lines while Hamas continued to launch rockets from Gaza.

9

Israel's ground and tunnel offensive

ISRAELI DECISION MAKERS, BOTH political and military, had been mulling the launch of a ground offensive in Gaza for several days; however, as mentioned earlier, for Israel, a ground offensive involving boots on the ground is a last resort action; a decision to send in troops would not be made unless absolutely necessary. In preparation for such an eventually the 40,000 reserve troops who had been called up and sent to the Gaza border remained on standby, joining tank and artillery brigades already there. As the rocket fire heated up a further 18,000 reserve soldiers were called up, which caused the Israeli populace to understand that a ground offensive was likely within days. At that time there were then 70,000 mobilized troops awaiting an order to enter Gaza.

Rocket barrages continued unabated and Israel's nuclear reactor in Dimona was targeted on two successive days. Two Unmanned Aerial Vehicles (UAVs) were launched from Gaza a few days apart; both were shot down by IAF fighter jets. Following that, Israel's worst fears were realized when 13 Hamas gunmen suddenly appeared out of a hole in the ground and set their sights on murdering and kidnapping Israelis in nearby kibbutz Sufa, which is south of the Gaza Strip. Fortunately, electronic warning devices alerted Israeli soldiers to the presence of terrorists and they engaged the gunmen in a firefight, killing two of them and wounding several others. The terrorists attempted to escape by crawling back to their tunnel entrance, but the Israelis had called for aerial backup and a helicopter soon appeared; it fired a missile into the group of gunmen scrambling for the tunnel entrance, which effectively ended that terror incursion.

Israel was well aware of the existence of underground tunnels beneath the Israel-Gaza border; one was effectively used by Hamas in June 2006 when gunmen exited a tunnel on the Israeli side of the border and attacked an IDF post. Two Hamas gunmen were killed as were two Israeli soldiers and another two Israelis were wounded. Hamas gunmen dragged one wounded Israeli soldier, Corporal Gilad Schalit (mentioned in part 1), back to Gaza via an underground tunnel. More than five years later, in October 2011, Schalit was swapped for over a thousand Palestinian terrorists that were being held in Israel prisons.

The July incursion into Israel by Hamas gunmen via an underground tunnel was the catalyst for an Israeli ground offensive. The IDF then had two objectives: to find and destroy Hamas's underground tunnels, and to destroy Hamas's capability to fire rockets into Israeli population centers. Following ten days of aerial bombardment the order was given on July 17 for troops to enter Gaza. At 10:38 p.m. tanks and Armored Personnel Carriers (APCs) entered Gaza and the hunt for terror tunnels began. The IDF released footage of an IDF captain giving a last minute briefing to the company he commands before they went into the Gaza Strip. The captain said:

> I don't think I need to explain to you why we are doing what we are doing. We are here in order to do what we trained for, and what we enlisted for—to protect the State of Israel, and to enable its right to exist in freedom, without them shooting mortars at us, and without us worrying about the families here on the border, and I am confident in what we are doing, because it is our right to be free in our land. It's not a slogan, it's the truth.

On the day the IDF began its ground offensive, Egyptian state news agency *MENA* reported that Sameh Shoukri, Egypt's foreign minister, had said that Hamas was at fault for the IDF's need to enter Gaza in a ground operation. "Had Hamas accepted the Egyptian proposal, it could have saved the lives of at least 40 Palestinians," Shoukri said. We know now that Hamas could have saved the lives of over 2,000 Palestinians had it accepted the ceasefire, but Hamas is always prepared to fight to the last drop of civilian blood while its leadership remains hunkered down in fortified bunkers or remain in their host-country's five-star hotels.

At this point it is worth repeating Hamas's July 10 statements regarding its use of human shields, which this writer used in part 3: Hamas spokesman Sami Abu Zuhri told the terrorist group's television station that "the tactic of using Gaza residents as human shields is praiseworthy and effective against Israel. This policy reflects the character of our brave, courageous people." Perhaps readers can now understand why so many Palestinians had been killed in Gaza. Israel warns Palestinian civilians of imminent danger if they do not vacate a building targeted for destruction, but Hamas orders them to remain in the buildings and the non-combatants die along with the combatants holed up in buildings that contain terror command centers and/or munitions.

Apparently, Egyptian leaders today are sensing that Hamas is a far greater threat to Egypt than Israel. According to *Associated French Press (AFP)*, on July 11 Egypt's security forces seized 20 Grad rockets being smuggled into the Sinai Peninsular from the Gaza Strip through a Palestinian tunnel under the Egyptian border. The rockets, along with their launch pads, were seized after a firefight between security forces and terrorists in the town of Rafah, which borders the Gaza enclave. The rockets were apparently meant to be used against Israel in attacks from the peninsula. Israel appreciated Egypt's contribution to the war against Hamas.

It is not only Hamas rockets that Israel had to contend with. Armed groups linked to Abu Mazen's (Mahmoud Abbas's) "moderate" Fatah movement has actively taken part in rocket attacks emanating from Gaza. The Nidal Al-Amody force of Fatah's Al-Aqsa Martyrs' Brigades claimed responsibility for firing Grad and other rockets toward Ashkelon, Sderot, Netivot, Kibbutz Ein Hashlosha, and the Sufa Crossing from out of Gaza. Communiques specifying the attacks were published on Fatah's official Facebook page. Early in the morning of July 17, another armed force associated with Fatah, the Abdul Qader Husseini Battalions, claimed responsibility for launching two Grad rockets at Ashkelon and four mortar shells at Kibbutz Nir Oz near Khan Yunis.

Worrying for Israel also were the rockets and mortars sporadically being fired into Israel from Lebanon, Syria, and the Sinai Peninsula. On the night of July 13 the IDF found itself responding with artillery fire for rockets fired from Syria at an IDF position on the Golan Heights. An IDF spokesman said the rockets were directly targeting Israel and were not stray fire from the conflict in Syria. The same day IAF jets struck three Syrian army positions, killing four and wounding ten others. The air attacks came in response to further rocket fire into the Golan Heights.

On July 14 Israel lodged a complaint with United Nations Secretary General Ban Ki-moon and the Security Council over sporadic rocket attacks from Lebanon directed at Israel. And on July 15 three Grad rockets were fired from Egypt's Sinai Peninsular into Elat, Israel's tourist mecca, injuring several people and damaging buildings and cars. Projectiles—rockets and mortars—were being fired into Israeli towns and cities from all around: from Gaza in the south, Lebanon in the north, Syria in the east, and from the Sinai Peninsular in the west. This persisted until the end of the war.

Apparently the days of conventional warfare on the battlefield are almost over. It is being replaced by aggressive missile warfare targeting civilians. Should Jesus delay His second coming mankind will eventually return itself to the stone age. In Israel's latest war with Hamas it appears that Hamas has already taken a giant leap back into the days of cavemen. Within five days of beginning its ground offensive IDF ground troops had already uncovered 35 complete tunnels with almost 100 entry and exit shafts.

In reality, Hamas's prolonged barrages of rockets and mortars did Israel a favor. Had Hamas used brains it would have withheld its rocket fire until after its planned mass infiltration into Israel by Hamas gunmen on Rosh HaShanah, the Jewish New Year. Israeli leaders knew about some of Hamas's terror tunnels prior to the ground offensive launched by the Israel Defense Forces (IDF) in July, but it was completely ignorant of the scope of the tunnel network despite all its media bluff and puff to the contrary. The IDF found an entire underground city—up to 112 feet (34 meters) beneath the surface—a miles/kilometers-long interlocking network of reinforced concrete and steel tunnels that has cost hundreds of millions of dollars and taken many years to build.

Finding the underground terror city was the first of a number of miracles that happened during Operation Protective Edge, which proves beyond doubt that *"the Lord of hosts, the Mighty One of Israel"* (Isaiah 1:24) still has His finger on Israel's pulse and is watching over it—*"He who keeps Israel neither slumbers nor sleeps"* (Psalms 121:4).

The IDF was deeply impressed with the quality of the tunnels, which resemble a giant underground maze. Following up on intelligence gathered from an informant, Faraj Abu Rabia, one of the architects of the Hamas tunnel effort, became a victim of an Israeli targeted assassination just before a ceasefire went into effect on August 11.

Hamas gunmen have been carrying out extensive military training in the tunnels and only those who are intimately familiar with the gargantuan maze can traverse the underground city of Gaza without coming to the surface. The tunnel city has electricity, a sewerage system, pumps to keep it free from water seepage, food, medicines, supplies of weaponry, multiples of concealed rocket launchers, and tranquilizers at the ready for subduing kidnapped Israelis.

Tunnel entrance and exit chutes are scattered throughout Gaza—hundreds of them—and the tunnels' main entrances are constructed under houses, mosques, schools, and hospitals. Many branches of the tunnels have exits inside Israel close to or actually within kibbutzim, schools, and kindergartens. Had the planned mass infiltration by Hamas gunmen taken place on Rosh HaShanah the Israeli civilian death toll would have been catastrophic; and the potential number of adults and children that could have been kidnapped simply boggles the mind.

The IDF believes it has destroyed all the tunnels leading into Israel, but given the large number of tributaries and exit chutes found that opened up inside Israel, this writer feels it is both premature and also naive to believe none have been missed. However, IDF troops should be applauded; they faced gunmen in civilian clothing, gunmen in women's clothing, and gunmen in IDF uniforms. They were the targets of snipers, IEDs (Improvised Explosive Devices), booby-trapped homes, booby-trapped schools, suicide bombers, and sophisticated weaponry. Gunmen popped out of tunnels, out of holes in walls, and even out of cupboards. The bravery of IDF soldiers is seemingly unmatched in warfare; they are courageous in the most daunting of conditions; the IDF often refers to its battle troops as "warriors." They do not fight for a cause like Hamas and such other groups; Israeli soldiers fight for the survival of their nation, period.

The IDF has progressed from being very much a people's army

in 1948 into one of Israeli society's most prominent institutions; it influences the economy, culture, and political scene—in 1965, the IDF was awarded the Israel Prize for its contribution to education. Today, only one in every two potential recruits is actually drafted for mandatory military service; gone are the days when practically everyone had to serve. The public's respect for its national guardian may seem excessive to some people living overseas; however, a person would need to reside in Israel for longer than a tourist visa allows, experience the constant threats that Israelis are forced to live under, before being able to really appreciate the IDF. The sense of camaraderie and loyalty that is intermingled between IDF troops and the general public has to be experienced to be believed. Two "lone soldiers"—soldiers without family in Israel—lost their lives in the recent war with Hamas; some 35,000 people turned out for the first funeral and around 12,000 for the second. Israelis did not want those boys to die and be buried without family—they became the boys' families out of respect and appreciation.

The attack tunnels are elaborate and large enough for motorcycles to be ridden through and for three men to stand side-by-side. One tunnel, which extended into Israel, contained two motorcycles; these were apparently about to be used in a surprise terror attack and also provide the terrorists with a quick getaway. Individual tunnels were discovered that were one mile (1.6 kilometers) in length and had multiple side branches with dozens of entrance and exit shafts. Many tunnels uncovered were virtually impervious to aerial assault unless bunker-buster bombs were used. Main entrances were most often found inside civilian houses, but they were also found within mosques and hospitals. The IDF believes that Hamas leaders were directing the rocket firings from one particular tunnel, which doubled as the Hamas war room and also their personal fortified bunker.

Many of the tunnel diggers were apparently children due to them being small and able to work in tight spaces. A 2012 article in the Journal of Palestine Studies claims that 160 Palestinian children died while working on Hamas's tunnel system. Adult tunnelers would work for many months on a single tunnel; they worked between eight and 12 hours each day for a monthly payment of between US$150 and US$300.

Israel obviously knew of the geographic locations of some tunnels through its spy network in Gaza, and also from its electronic surveillance methods. It had also been made painfully aware of the existence of the tunnels from the virtual knowledge learned through the Hamas cross-border attack in June 2006 when Hamas terrorists emerged from a tunnel inside Israel near an IDF post, killed two Israeli soldiers and dragged a wounded soldier back into Gaza through the tunnel. That unfortunate soldier, Corporal Gilad Schalit, remained a Hamas captive for five years and four months before being finally released in a swap for 1,027 Palestinian prisoners. This therefore begs the question of why the IDF was not ordered to destroy the tunnels earlier rather than let them lie fallow and be responsible for the death of 11 more IDF soldiers? This is sure to be one of the questions that will require answering during the probe into the shortcomings of Operation Protective Edge, a probe that was ordered even before Israel's ground offensive was launched.

As stated above, Israel obviously knew of the locations of some tunnels, but it was certainly ignorant of the extent of the underground city due to Hamas's security measures that are used to keep the tunnels a secret. An August 10 report on the IDF's website told how Hamas gunmen killed dozens of the diggers responsible for the extensive tunnel system. During the previous few weeks, fearing the tunnelers would reveal the locations to Israel, Hamas gunmen shot anyone they suspected might transfer tunnel information to Israel. A former tunnel digger—an actual Israeli collaborator—told the website that Hamas would strip search the workers to ensure they had no recording devices or cameras hidden on them. He said:

> The people we met had their faces covered, no one knew them by their real names, it was all codes and first names. They didn't want to take the risk that some of the diggers were collaborating with Israel.

Sources in Gaza say Hamas took a series of precautions to prevent information from reaching Israel. The terror organization would blindfold the diggers going to and from the sites in order to prevent them from recognizing the locations. The tunnels were evidently very strictly supervised by Hamas gunmen; civilians were kept far from the sites. After the tunnels were completed, dozens of tunnelers were executed to prevent intelligence leaks to Israel. One source said:

> Anyone they suspected might transfer information on the tunnels to Israel was killed by the Hamas military wing. They were very cruel.

On August 19 Hamas took a *Reuters* crew into one of its tunnels, ostensibly to show the world that Israel had not destroyed all its tunnels. The *Reuters* crew was blindfolded and driven, with a few twists and turns in between, to a tunnel where the gunmen boasted that Hamas was "restocking its arsenal of rockets and other weaponry and shoring up its underground network." One of the gunmen said, "In peace we make preparations, and in war we use what we have readied." However, with the crew blindfolded there was no way of telling whether the tunnel actually went under Israel's border as was claimed by the gunmen.

By the IDF's own admission, Israel's ground forces only focused on destroying tunnels within a 2 – 4.5 kilometer (1.25 – 2.8 mile) proximity of Israel's border; the troops ignored more distant connecting passages. At this point the IDF forces had destroyed 34 tunnels, 14 of which went under Israel's border and exited in or near populated areas. The end of one tunnel was stacked with explosives—directly under an Israeli kindergarten.

10

Death and destruction from air, sea, and land

ISRAEL'S OPERATION PROTECTIVE EDGE that was waged against Hamas's rocket-fire into Israeli cities and towns and which was a fight against Hamas terrorists in Gaza, had entered its sixteenth day; it was then day seven of Israel's ground offensive.

Terrible destruction was being wreaked in Gaza as the IAF targeted Hamas lairs, which often caused massive secondary explosions as weapons caches ignited. Israel's Navy was also pounding Hamas targets with precision ordinances from the sea. Israeli troops were moving house to house in Gaza City seeking out the entrances to Hamas "attack tunnels," gunmen, and weapons caches. When Israeli troops uncovered a tunnel entrance they entered the tunnel and often engaged in fierce fighting with Hamas gunmen who desperately tried to protect their tunnels. The "attack tunnels," as they are now being called, had taken years to dig and fortify, each tunnel costing millions of dollars to construct; they are all interconnected, like a huge network of nerves and arteries. There is a virtual city beneath Gaza, a labyrinth, which to the IDF resembles a maze. There is one Gaza City above ground and another city beneath the ground.

The tunnels had been dubbed "attack tunnels" due to the fact that 30 tunnels had by this time been discovered that went right under the Gaza-Israel border and came out near, and often inside, Israeli towns and kibbutzim. High-ranking IDF officers said that the tunnels are impressive. One suggested in a quip that Israel should "employ the tunnelers to build the proposed underground light rail in Tel Aviv." Israeli demolition experts destroy the tunnels with explosives. Often, when munitions inside the tunnel ignites the secondary explosion sends rubble and earth several hundred meters (yards) into the air.

Several incursions into Israel by dozens of Hamas gunmen wearing IDF uniforms had taken place in the preceding few days; the intent was one of murder and the kidnapping of Israelis. Fortunately, IDF troops in full combat gear were swarming around near the Gaza border and all attempts to kill or kidnap Israelis ended either in the deaths of the gunmen or of them fleeing back to the safety of their underground fortresses. The "attack tunnels" that were discovered running under the border could have accommodated an invasion force into southern Israel of at least 1,000 fully armed terrorists, which could have created a massacre of cosmic proportions among the Israeli population of southern Israel.

The fiercest fighting in Gaza took place around the tunnel entrances and a heavy casualty toll was taken among the Israeli soldiers with 32 having fallen in battle at this point in the war. The terrorist gunmen had the advantage over the Israeli soldiers; they waited in ambush and would suddenly pop out of one of the concealed tunnel exits that the Israelis were searching for. Deaths among Hamas gunmen slowly inched up due to fierce firefights around the tunnel entrances. At this point in the operation some 75 gunmen had surrendered to Israeli troops, another 31 had been captured; all were interrogated at a detention center within Israel.

Israeli border towns emptied out as the battles beyond the border raged and infiltrations by Hamas gunmen appeared to be on the rise. Fifty percent of the residents of Israel's southern communities had by now gone to live elsewhere; the number rose to 80 percent in towns that abutted the Gaza border. Southern border town residents were seeking safer ground; the newly discovered "attack tunnels" had them spooked. Ofra Benudiz, a mother of four, living in a kibbutz near Sderot, said:

> It's changed our viewpoint entirely. The rockets we somehow got used to. This is something else. They are under our homes. Our greatest fear is that they will infiltrate.

Others told of how, when they closed their eyes at night, they heard "phantom shoveling sounds." It was a rude awakening for them to realize later that the noises were actual and not phantom.

One tunnel came out right under the dining room of a kibbutz. Had gunmen broken out of that tunnel there would have been many casualties.

IDF troops had fought ferocious firefights with Hamas gunmen who knew every inch of the tunnels; the soldiers found that the really fierce fighting took place when gunmen fought to protect Hamas command centers. The IDF was still looking for the master tunnel that houses the Hamas high command.

On Monday July 21, after four days of advance warning for Palestinians to leave their homes in the Shejaiya neighborhood of Gaza City, Israel attacked the Hamas stronghold with ferocity. That day Israel lost 13 of its soldiers, and some 80 Palestinians were also killed. Gallagher Fenwick, the correspondent for *France24*, followed the Hamas line and parroted about a massacre of women and children. Fenwick and others would be unable to broadcast from Gaza if they did not toe the Hamas media line, but watching *France24* news—which at the best of times is little less than a mouthpiece for the Palestinians; always pro-Palestinian and always biased against Israel—Fenwick's terrorist-line monologues were to be expected. Conversely, *Al-Jazeera*, which has been, and is repeatedly labeled, a "terrorist network," was far more accurate in its English news broadcasts, even reporting that most of the Palestinians killed were of fighting age.

Hamas had ordered all Palestinian media and social networking sites to always use the term "innocent civilians" when referring to casualties and they were "not to show evidence of rockets fired from population centers." However, several foreign correspondents did tweet that rockets were being fired from near their hotels, and one tweet told of a Hamas gunman going through the Shejaiya neighborhood of Gaza City "dressed in a woman's headscarf ... tip of a gun poked out from under cloak." The tweeting correspondents all received threats on their lives; but one, Harry Fear, a journalist from the UK, tweeted his critics:

> Should a journalist only report the noise and ferocity of Israel's attacks & not the sounds of Gaza's rockets? Both terrify people.

IDF soldiers suffered heavy losses fighting in Shejaiya due to being fired upon by some 900 gunmen from more than 20 houses with machine guns, rocket propelled grenades, and anti-tank weapons. They entered houses looking for tunnel entrances and found many booby-trapped buildings, some of which exploded, bringing the building down upon the soldiers' heads. Several attack tunnels were found that led from Shejaiya right to the Israeli border, a distance of almost two and a half kilometers (1.5 miles). Inside the tunnels were found tranquilizers and bandages, which would likely have been in preparation for kidnappings.

The IDF released audio and video recordings of the warnings being given to civilian residents in Gaza City. The IDF actually counts the number of people who flee from a particular building after a warning is issued. According to the size of the building being targeted, if the number of those running out is not large enough the IAF either drops a dummy bomb on the building, known colloquially as a "knock on the roof," or drops a small bomb onto the roof of the building as a warning; watching the maneuver this writer then saw more people run out of a building. After a few moments a warplane dropped a one ton bomb and the building erupted in a terrifying, massive fireball when the munitions inside exploded. When the rubble and dust settle and the smoke drifted away, the building was nowhere to be seen.

The IAF pilots had been flying sorties almost non-stop for 16 days and often could only nap in their planes; some had not seen their wives or children for several days at a time. Pilots interviewed by Israel's *Channel 2* television told how they had difficulty sleeping after they inadvertently kill civilians.

On the evening of July 7 the IDF released black-and-white aerial footage of a site in the Gaza Strip which was marked as a target for the IAF to attack. The footage was for Israeli consumption, but it was an example of the lengths Israel went to in order to save Palestinian lives.

The video shows the target, but as the Israeli pilot zeroed in on the target, he stopped short of dropping munitions on it, as he had been instructed to do. "There are people; there are people close to our target," he could be heard saying in Hebrew. "It looks like there are people, possibly children, in our targeted area." After a moment, he receives a reply from the personnel on the ground. "We are not going to strike this target now," says a female soldier on the other end of the line. "Let's move on."

Those political talking heads screaming for Israel to end its hostilities against Hamas would do well to ascertain exactly what is going on instead of spouting about what they do not know. Does the reader not think it odd that Israel is the only nation that is not allowed to win? Europe, especially, seems to believe that Israelis should be happy to be fodder for terrorist rockets, but then the great majority of Europeans are inherently anti-Semitic. Anti-Israelism is merely a euphemism for anti-Semitism.

11

Carnage in Gaza

ISRAEL'S OPERATION PROTECTIVE EDGE had entered its 18th day. The carnage being inflicted upon Gazans continued unabated, as did the rocket fire into Israel from Hamas's underground launchers. Were it not for the tens of thousands of bomb shelters and mandatory safe rooms in Israel, to which Israeli's can flee the incoming rockets, there would have been massive casualties among the Israeli population. The Iron Dome missile defense system is the hero of Israel's Home Front; T-shirts, hats, and tote-bags bearing its image are to be seen everywhere.

The carnage in Gaza would have been substantially less if Hamas had not barbarically used the Gazan population as human shields as a defence against IDF attacks. This writer has previously written about Hamas's boast that human shields are "effective" against Israel. Hamas wanted "telegraphic" bodies to show the world on its television screens—the more bodies the better. Hamas leaders have stated that they will fight to the last drop of blood, but with Hamas kingpin Khaled Mashaal hanging out in a five-star hotel in Qatar—a guest of Sheikh Hamad bin-Khalifa Al-Thani, the Emir of Qatar, who is Hamas's terror financier—and other Hamas bigwigs either in similar surroundings in Istanbul, London, Beirut, and other cities, or hiding themselves in fortified command bunkers underground in Gaza, it is quite obvious that they actually mean they will continue to fight to the last drop of Gazan civilian blood.

Up until this point in time two rocket caches had already been discovered in United Nations Relief and Works Agency (UNRWA) schools. The first cache was handed back to Hamas authorities and the second cache "disappeared" before it could be formerly handed back to Hamas. Another UNRWA school was hit by projectiles on July 24 killing 15 adults and children and injuring around 200. At that time of writing the blog post the IDF was conducting an investigation into the tragedy, but no one, including UN Secretary General Ban Ki-moon who was in the region, knows who carried out the attack. The IDF said that it came under fire from a position near the school and fired back at the position, but it also said Hamas fired into that area and may have hit the school. It would also not be beyond the realms of comprehension that Hamas fighters may have deliberately targeted the school in order to bring condemnation upon Israel; it had committed such atrocities in past conflicts with Israel.

On July 23 the IDF blew up sections of the Al-Wafa rehabilitation hospital in Gaza's Shejaiya neighborhood. The medical facility was being used as a Hamas command center and was used repeatedly by Hamas gunmen to launch attacks on Israeli forces. After ensuring that patients had been moved elsewhere and that the hospital warden assured the IDF that the complex was empty apart from active gunmen and that the doors were locked, Israeli demolition experts set charges and blew up the hospital. The IDF later released a video showing gunfire emanating from several window openings in the premises; the video also showed a Hamas tunnel opening adjacent to the hospital. Another video with full audio showed heavy fighting in the Shejaiya neighborhood and a spotter was telling the Israeli soldiers how many Hamas gunmen were leaving a particular building. The spotter's voice-level rose as he said, "two of them have just stopped an ambulance and gotten into it—they are south-bound in an ambulance." Israeli forces did not strike the ambulance due to the possibility of it carrying civilian non-combatants.

Hamas is guilty of a very long list of war crimes and crimes against humanity, but it was Israel that got condemned on a daily basis. There were tens of thousands of protestors around the world demonstrating against Israel. Where were the outraged demonstrators protesting against the 200,000 plus deaths in the Syrian conflict? Where was the outrage and demonstrations against the cold blooded murders of hundreds of sunni soldiers in Iraq by ISIS? Where are the demonstrations and outrage over the shooting down of the Malaysian passenger jet over the Ukraine? This writer could go on and on, but the truth of the matter is that there are only large demonstrations and outrage when the object of the hatred is Israel.

London is now close to being 70 percent Muslim and tens of thousands of them turned out to vent their hatred of Israel in demonstrations. The same was true in Paris, which has a huge population of Muslims; more French Jews are making aliyah to Israel than at anytime since the founding of the state in 1948—they are running for their lives out of an anti-Semitic France. Houston, Texas, saw 900 people protesting against Israel; again, the majority were Muslim. Turkey had tens of thousands screaming against Israel. Prime Minister Recep Tayyip Erdoğan is slowly turning Turkey into a radical Islamic state and he hates Israel even more than Adolf Hitler hated Jews.

The stupidity and ignorance of Western leaders who opened their nation's doors to Muslim immigration has also opened the way for Islam to take over their nations, and it will. Islam will sort the Christian sheep from the "Christian" goats; the Christian wheat from the "Christian" chaff. Christ will have a purified Church to return to, and it is this writer's belief that Islam will lead the way in that purifying process. Meanwhile, Israel, the nation state of God's chosen people, has to do battle with fanatical Islamist terrorists who want to eradicate it from the face of the earth.

There are two score of people in the interactive unit of the Israel Defense Forces. They pump out missives using social media in six languages in a tone much punchier than the typical news release, e.g. "Israel uses the Iron Dome to protect its civilians. Hamas uses civilians to protect its rockets." While this is an absolutely 100 percent correct assessment, some of the civilian social media postings, usually from teenagers on both sides, are dehumanizing to say the least. Those Palestinians that murdered the three Israeli teenagers were called "beasts" and "animals." However, as this writer has pointed out, the Jews that murdered the Arab teenager were no less "animals" than the Arab murderers. As horrendous as both these murders were there is still no justification for either side calling for the "extermination" of the other. Hatred and racism has no place in civilized society. Barbarianism only breeds barbarianism.

12

Gaza destruction and Hamas terror tunnels

ALL INTERNATIONAL TELEVISION NEWS networks were showing video clips of the devastation that Israel had wrought upon Gazan communities. Wide areas of the Hanoun and Shejaiya neighborhoods have been reduced to humongous piles of rubble. It must seem to Western television viewers that Israel is just a callous monster that has absolutely no regard for Palestinian life. Watching these clips and listening to the majority of the accompanying audios from reporters it is as if the poor Palestinians had done nothing to warrant such indiscriminate destruction. The majority of the foreign reporters limited their reporting to what the Palestinians were suffering; there was barely a mention of the reasons for the havoc that had befallen their towns and Gaza City. It is all about what Israel had done and nothing about the reason why Israel had been forced to level huge swathes of Palestinian population areas.

First of all, reporters were not allowed to report anything except the Hamas line, which is that Israel is the aggressor and casualties are all civilians; the great majority being women and children. Any reporter that did not follow the Hamas line was not allowed to report, period. Reporters who would not follow the Hamas propaganda line had been confined to their hotels and were prevented from leaving Gaza. Hamas gained bonus sympathy points when reporters were killed while locked into Gaza as air and artillery strikes were being carried out.

Second of all, and most importantly, Hamas had been firing rockets from between homes in the devastated neighborhoods and Israel had been targeting those rocket launching sites. On top of the crime of firing missiles from populated areas, Hamas has also constructed a labyrinth of what is now called "attack" or "terror" tunnels. This tunnel network runs beneath the neighborhoods and extend under Israel's border and exit inside Israel, either near or inside Israel kibbutzim and moshavim. Some of these tunnels, those nearest to the Israeli border, are only hundreds of meters in length while many are a kilometer or two in length; the longest tunnel discovered thus far is two and one half kilometers (1.55 miles) in length. Israel had by now discovered more than 45 tunnels, each of which has side tunnels that connect to other tunnels, and each has a multiple of exit and entrance chutes. Israel has demolished many of these tunnels by drilling down at variously set distances through the 18–30 plus meters (yards) of earth and reinforced concrete and inserted explosives, which, when detonated, creates a massive kilometers-long explosion. It is unfortunate that houses and buildings often straddled the tunnels and were also reduced to rubble; however, the residents were given warnings that they needed to leave in order to not be harmed. This was standard procedure when Israel was about to attack a weapons cache or destroy tunnels that run under the neighborhood. Some Palestinians heeded Israel's warnings and some opted to heed Hamas's order to remain in their homes to act as human shields.

While half of all Palestinian casualties were fighting-age males, and hundreds had been positively identified as Hamas gunmen, which made their deaths legitimate, the death toll is exaggerated by the fact that civilians have no bomb shelters to which they can run. Hamas used almost all its billions of dollars in funds, cement, and reinforcing steel that Israel had allowed into the Gaza Strip to build its terror tunnels. Israel's military engineers estimate that each tunnel costs several millions of dollars to build and contains an aggregate of 800 tons of concrete. For this reason Gaza lacks hospitals, schools, and the like because Hamas, the ruling body in Gaza, made terror tunnels and weaponry its top priority.

If Israel does not locate and destroy these terror tunnels, which also double as underground launch sites for the more than 2,260 rockets thus far fired into Israel since July 6, it will be forced to launch another invasion of Gaza in a year or two or three when Hamas has regrouped and rearmed and begins another round of rocket fire and terror infiltrations against the Israeli population. Only next time it will be with more powerful rockets that will have longer ranges. The IDF must destroy these attack tunnels if Israelis are not to live in perpetual fear of terrorist rocket attacks or terrorist infiltrations from Gaza. At this stage of the war, within the past few days six Israeli soldiers had been killed by gunmen emerging from tunnels inside Israel. One tunnel discovered ended directly below an Israeli kindergarten; it was packed with explosives in preparation for decimating the kindergarten and butchering all the children. Another tunnel discovered was full of maps and IDF uniforms. The maps clearly indicated, and was later confirmed through interrogation of captured gunmen, that on Rosh HaShanah (Jewish New Year), which would fall on September 25, there was to be a mass infiltration of gunmen into Israel to commit murder and mayhem in Israel's southern towns. Hamas actually did Israel a favor when it began firing hundreds of rockets every day into Israel, prompting Israel's ground offensive and the discovery of the dozens of attack tunnels. The ground offensive had effectively stymied Hamas's plans for mass infiltrations into Israel over the holiday period.

When the reader next sees television footage of the destruction in Gaza, the reader would do well to give a little thought to the fact that all the destruction has not happened due to a mere whim of the Israeli military. The Palestinians have brought it upon themselves by allowing Hamas to use their homes for entrances to the underground city of terror tunnels. For this, many Palestinians received payment, but many were just willing to look the other way. The Palestinians have also allowed Hamas to use civilian apartment buildings and public amenities to store their munitions, which had been detonated either by Israelis soldiers or by an IAF missile. The destruction in Gaza is indeed colossal.

13

The toppling of Hamas (1)

ON JULY 27, 2014, several Israeli newspapers carried a *Reuters* inspired article that warned Israel against trying to topple the Hamas terror organization, against which Israel is waging its third war in six years. The headline on the article carried by *The Times of Israel* was:

US intel official warns against toppling Hamas

The article's s sub-heading read:

Outgoing DIA head Michael Flynn says removing Gaza ruling group could make way for Islamic State

The writers, Lazar Berman, together with *Times of Israel* staff, said, Quote:

> Speaking at a high-level security conference in Aspen, Colorado, outgoing US Defense Intelligence Agency head Michael Flynn warned against the dangers of toppling Hamas, saying what may replace the Islamist group could be even worse.
>
> 'If Hamas were destroyed and gone, we would probably end up with something much worse. The region would end up with something much worse,' Flynn, a lieutenant general, told the conference Saturday, according to *Reuters*.
>
> He warned that with Hamas out of the picture, the Islamic State, or something like the brutal Islamist group ruling over parts of Syria and Iraq, could take its place.
>
> Flynn also said that he was pessimistic about the Middle East's future. 'Is there going to be a peace in the Middle East? Not in my lifetime,' he said.

In June, Egypt arrested 15 men it said belonged to the Islamic State as they crossed from Rafah [in Gaza] into the Sinai Peninsula. In addition, videos have emerged on YouTube showing masked men pledging allegiance to IS [Islamic State] and firing rockets at Israel.

Hamas denies the presence of IS members in the Gaza Strip. Unquote.

Michael Flynn postulates that should Israel topple Hamas it could end up with a worse terror group in the Strip. This writer wonders on which planet Flynn had been living?

Amos Yadlin, Israel's former military intelligence head, who is currently the head of the Institute for National Security Studies in Tel Aviv, said categorically in an unrelated interview, "I don't see any alternative that will be worse than Hamas."

Hamas is the Palestinian offshoot of the Egyptian Muslim Brotherhood, whose goal is to establish an Islamic state to replace Israel. Amos Yadlin accurately represents the sentiments of both the upper echelons of Israel's political scene, and also the top brass of Israel's military. What Flynn, President Barack Obama, US Secretary of State John Kerry, the EU, and others do not want to hear or acknowledge is that Israel has the equivalent of ISIL (Islamic State in Iraq and the Levant), now known as Islamic State since its declaration of it being the new Muslim caliphate on June 29, 2014, on its very doorstep. Only the IDF has prevented Hamas and it jihadist partners, like the Palestinian Islamic Jihad and the Popular Front for the Liberation of Palestine (PLFP), from sneaking into Israel and butchering every living Israeli.

The United States, led by the racist, closet Muslim, Barack Hussein Obama, set fires throughout the Middle East before retreating back to its armchair to tell the world how to deal with problems that itself, with all its military might, has been unable to solve. In six short years America has evolved from being the greatest global power into just being a great global nuisance.

Looking to Obama to deal with global Islam will only find him bowing down to Muslim kings and kissing the hands and robes of Muslim sheiks; he makes excuses for Islamic murderers at home and exchanges an American traitor in Afghanistan for five powerful, murderous Taliban leaders—one of whom was a key player in the 9/11 attacks upon America—and who had been captured by US forces and imprisoned in Guantanamo Bay. And this Obama did while keeping his mouth tightly shut about the plight of a Christian woman, Merriam Ibrahim, who was sentenced first to be lashed 100 times and then hung for the unpardonable crime of being a Christian. Ibrahim, the wife of an American citizen and eight-months pregnant, refused to recant her faith in Jesus. For this she was sentenced to death. She was incarcerated in a Sudanese prison along with her 20-month-old son Martin and gave birth to a daughter, Maya, in prison. Only the outpouring of justifiable outrage from around the world managed to release Ibrahim from her dreadful ordeal. Sudanese authorities said that "the West needed to respect the laws of Sudan;" however, the only Westerner that apparently respects the draconian laws of Sudan is Barry Obama. Had Ibrahim been a Muslim he would have mounted his horse and charged straight into battle, but she was a Christian and Christians do not matter to the one who thinks "It's All About Me" and sits on the throne in the White House.

The fanatical Islamic Republic of Iran, whom Obama is about set to appease through negotiations over Iran's nuclear weapons program, has been arming Hamas for years and is easily the worlds number one fomenter of terrorism. Iran has repeatedly called for Israel to "wiped off the map" and on July 27, 2014, Brigadier-General Hossein Salami, the deputy commander of Iran's Revolutionary Guards, said that Israelis "are trees without roots," which were planted in Islamic lands by the British—a reference to the Balfour Declaration, which led to the eventual creation of the state of Israel in 1948. Salami said his troops would "hunt down Israelis house to house," that Israel "must be wiped from the face of the Earth." Salami went on to say, "The end of the Zionist regime has arrived. Islamic movements are armed, missiles are positioned, and today we witness how the arms of the resistance in a corner of the Islamic world are controlling events"—referring to both Hamas in Gaza and the Islamic State in Iraq and Syria.

The newly declared Sunni Islamic caliphate already says its empire straddles two countries, extending from Diyala in Iraq to Aleppo in Syria. It claims that Abu Bakr al-Baghdadi is IS's leader and caliph of all Muslims everywhere, and that al-Baghdadi is the direct descendent of Muhammed, the founder of Islam. Abu Mohamed al-Adnani is the Islamic State's spokesman and he calls upon all Muslims to swear allegiance to the new caliph and he indicates further expansion of the caliphate:

> The legality of all emirates, groups, states and organizations becomes null by the expansion of the caliph's authority and the arrival of its troops to their areas. Listen to your caliph and obey him. Support your state, **which grows every day** (this writer's emphasis).

It is the growing every day that should concern all Western nations, not just Israel. The name of the Islamic State prior to taking that name was ISIL—Islamic State in Iraq and the Levant. The Levant today consists of Israel, the Palestinian territories, Jordan, Lebanon, Syria, Cyprus, and southern Turkey (the former Aleppo Vilayet). A large part of Iraq is under IS control as is a the large adjoining area of Syria. There are some 1,100 Islamic groups in Syria that are fighting against Syrian President Bashar Assad and also fighting against each other. The most powerful jihadi group in Syria is linked to IS and has virtually vanquished all the other groups, which have now retreated to the eastern part of Syria. At the time of writing IS is well on its way to taking all of Syria.

A coalition of Western nations led by the US began striking ISIS from the air in Iraq in August 2014 and in Syria in September 2014; however, following weeks of continuous airstrikes the advance of the jihadists, which had momentarily slowed with the first few strikes, has since freshened and ISIS is daily taking new territory in both countries, expanding its control rather than contracting.

Hamas in Gaza is ideologically identical to ISIS and equally as murderous. It is only the IDF that keeps it from murdering all Israelis. Under interrogation, a captured Hamas gunman unwittingly told his Israeli captors of a second miracle; following is his statement—very little had been leaked to the press in order to prevent possible panic among Israelis:

> For twelve years we have been building these tunnels and waiting for the right moment, when we were trained and ready. We decided that the time would be

this year on Rosh Hashanah, 2014. We chose Rosh Hashanah because most of the soldiers get leave to go home and there aren't a lot on guard duty, and it's a two-day holiday. All of Hamas would go through the tunnels we've built over twelve years and capture Israel. In every tunnel we'd send two, three dozen armed men and kidnap civilians, women, children, and bring them back to Gaza through the tunnels. And then Israel couldn't bomb the tunnels because of all the Israeli civilians inside them. And in this way we would occupy the entire country and rule Israel and kill all the Zionists. For years we were planning this and it was going to happen in two months. Your attacks on Gaza destroyed our plans.

How true is God's promise to Israel: *He who keeps Israel shall neither slumber nor sleep* (Psalms 121:4. Our God knew all along about Hamas's plan and nudged Hamas into foolishly sending thousands of rockets into Israeli towns and cities, which forced Israel to first pound Gaza from the air to lessen the rocket fire and to destroy Hamas's infrastructure. A few infiltrations by Hamas gunmen into Israel prodded the IDF into a ground offensive, which has uncovered the extent of Hamas's underground terror city. Perhaps the reader can now understand why Israel bucked the world's condemnation of its actions in Gaza, determined not to stop until the terror tunnel city has been destroyed. It has finally become apparent to one or two of the world's leaders that Gaza must be demilitarized, but as Amos Yadlin said on July 27:

> Asking Hamas to demilitarize Gaza is like asking a priest to convert to Judaism. They will not demilitarize Gaza voluntarily, the only one who can demilitarize them is the IDF.

Many in Israel think the only way to demilitarize Gaza is by Israel reoccupying it like it occupied it in 1967 during the Six-Day War.

14

The toppling of Hamas (2)

AT THE TIME THIS blog post was originally written the number of Palestinians killed in Israel's recent war against Hamas had reached well beyond 1,400 in 24 days of fighting, with more than 6,000 wounded. The IDF believed it had killed around 1,000 Hamas terrorists (which would underline Israeli claims that there is a far higher proportion of combatants than widely reported among the 1,400 plus Gaza fatalities cited by Gazan health sources); 61 Israeli soldiers and three civilians had been killed. Hamas had fired over 2,800 rockets into Israel at this point, and had attempted eight attacks through cross-border tunnels, killing 11 IDF soldiers.

President Obama and John Kerry his secretary of state have turned to Qatar and Turkey to mediate between Israel and Hamas. In a telephone call between Prime Minister Netanyahu and Obama, Netanyahu objected to the use of Turkey and Qatar; Netanyahu said, "Turkey and Qatar are Hamas's biggest supporters and they can't be relied upon to act as fair interlocutors." Obama retorted, "I trust Qatar and Turkey, Israel is not at all in the position to choose its mediators." Of course Obama trusts Qatar and Turkey, the leaders of those countries are radical Islamists and are particular buddies of his. Obama has appointed five Muslims to head departments in his administration and he is slowly bringing others around to his way of thinking about Muslims.

On July 28 House Minority Leader Nancy Pelosi said the United States must look to Qatar, an ally of Hamas, for advice in resolving the Palestinian-Israeli conflict. That is like getting a hyena to mediate between a fox and the chickens in a hen house. Pelosi also said to CNN's Candy Crowley, "we have to confer with the Qataris, who have told me over and over again that Hamas is a humanitarian organization." As the old adage goes, "There's one born every minute." A humanitarian organization? Israeli leaders and the IDF's top brass consider Hamas to be "the embodiment of Islamic extremist evil."

A video, broadcast on Hamas's *Al-Aqsa TV* station, and made available by the Middle East Media Research Institute (*MEMRI*), shows a Hamas-affiliated Imam conducting a sermon at a mosque in Dir al-Balah in the central Gaza Strip. Addressing Israelis the cleric says:

> Our doctrine in fighting you is that we will totally exterminate you. We will not leave a single one of you alive, because you are alien usurpers of the land and eternal mercenaries.

Israeli Foreign Minister Avigdor Liberman says, "What is happening today in the Middle East is a 'clash of civilizations' between the free world and radical Islam." And this is borne out by Hamas's military chief Muhammad Deif. In his first recording in 12 years Deif declares that Hamas will prevail in its struggle against Israel because its fighters "are eager for death" while Israel's "are eager for life."

ISIS Jihadists, besides murdering hundreds upon hundreds of Iraqi Shia soldiers, are also murdering the Iraqi Christians and driving them out of their ancient Christian communities where they have lived for nearly 2,000 years. Like some Christians in Syria, thousands of Iraqi Christians still speak Aramaic, but the butchering, beheadings, and expulsions by Islamists is also taking place throughout Syria. As one analyst said, "In our lifetimes we may well see the end of Christianity in the places where it began."

What is taking place in the Middle East is indeed a clash of civilizations and Israel was the only nation standing against the Islamic jihadists at that time. For taking this stand Israel was pilloried by almost the entire Western world, which only goes to prove how naive and anti-Semitic the West really is. Israel is not fighting for a cause it is fighting for survival and it will thumb its nose at all the Western leaders who demand a cessation of its war against Hamas. Unlike other wars, in which America has usually blackmailed Israel into pulling back its troops, this war saw Obama holding up deliveries of Hellfire air-to-ground missiles and also tank shells to Israel; nevertheless the war will not be over until Israel decides it is over and on its own terms.

Netanyahu has dared to publicly contradict Obama before the media, and in the first week of August tensions between Netanyahu and US Secretary of State John Kerry boiled over in a telephone call and there was a "disconnect." The call was abruptly ended and neither man spoke to the other for some time after their altercation. Netanyahu also reprimanded Washington by admonishing Dan Shapiro, the US ambassador to Israel, "not to second-guess him again" over Israel's policy toward Hamas. There is a considerable amount of bad blood between Netanyahu and the Obama administration; under Netanyahu's leadership Israel does not come to heel when Obama jerks the chain.

Netanyahu is open to a ceasefire-arrangement, providing the agreement makes provision for Israel to continue with the destruction of Hamas terror tunnels and makes no provision for Hamas to rebuild them or to rearm. On July 31 Israel had called up an additional 18,000 reservists, bringing the total number of mobilized reservists to 86,000. Adding this number of reservists to the standing army showed that Netanyahu had little or no faith for a lasting ceasefire. Hamas had quickly broken all five of the earlier ceasefires and will just a quickly break the next one.

This latest war will not topple Hamas, but it will wound it so severely that it will take years for it to recover and then Israel will have to "mow the grass" again, which is an IDF term for its many skirmishes against Hamas. Israel, according to Professor Efraim Inbar, the head of Bar Ilan University's Begin Sadat Center for Strategic Studies, is in a "protracted intractable conflict." Inbar says he has "psychological difficulties digesting the facts that there is no solution in sight." Gaza will continue to be Gaza, many challenges lie ahead for Israel. It is Israel's lot to be situated, by God's design, in the very heart of the Islamic heartland.

Arabs are fighting Arabs, jihadists fighting jihadists, Sunni Muslims fighting Shia Muslims, and both Sunni and Shia Muslims fighting Alawite Muslims. What is the reason for all this bad blood? This writer would here like to include an excerpt from what he first wrote two years ago for an issue of the *Update*, the newsletter of the Arm of Salvation ministries:

When will Western politicians stop making excuses for Islam, and stop referring to Muslim jihadi terrorists as a small fringe group. According to world experts this 'fringe group' is numbered in the millions—up to 130 million fanatical murderers. Western politicians need to refrain from calling Islam a 'peaceful religion' when in reality it is nothing less than a murderous religion spawned by Satan. Politicians who call Islam a 'peaceful religion' need to have their heads boiled in oil in order to soften them up. Those who opine such naiveté only broadcast their propensity to appease the Muslim world due to fear of jihadi reprisals. Make no mistake, Islam is a brutal, savage religion, and one only has to look at the atrocities being carried out by Islamists on every continent to understand the truth of this fact. And it is the Qu'ran, Islam's holy book, that fuels both Islamic bigotry, Islam's savagery, and Islam's oppression of and cruelty to females. No one is safe from the millions of jihadists who are endeavoring to carry out the Qu'ran's instruction: 'Prepare to strike terror into the hearts of the enemies of Allah' (Sura 8:60).

Just like Darwin's Origin of the Species, which has been rammed down our children's throats and called Evolution, so has Allah, the demonic spirit that rules Islam, been transformed into a pseudo-respectable immortal and is daily reported by the simpleton leftist mainstream media to actually be God—the God of Creation, the Bible, and Israel. However, Allah is a particular name for a particular Islamic spirit—it is NOT the God of Creation, the Bible, or Israel. School teachers have indoctrinated the world's children with the theory of evolution and the gullible leftist mainstream media pedals Allah as God hundreds of times every day and has brainwashed the Western world's masses. Daily we read of the Lebanese terrorist group Hizb'allah as being Hezbollah or Hizb'allah, but Allah is Allah and Hizb'allah is the party of Allah. Who has ever heard of anyone worshiping Ollah or Ullah? Such spellings are but figments of the media's overly fertile imagination; only ignorant newspaper editors and broadcasters will promote such names in order to be politically correct.

Arabs everywhere are fighting and killing anyone that does not agree with them. The Bible tells us that Ishmael, and by extension, his kith and kin:

'will be a wild donkey a of a man; his hand will be against everyone and everyone's hand against him, and he will live in hostility toward all his brothers' (Genesis 16:12).

How true that has turned out to be. And of course, Islam was spawned by a genocidal jihadist Arab named Mohammad who exported his demonic religion far beyond Arabia's borders. Thus, today, we have millions of genocidal jihadists whose hands are against their brothers everywhere; butchering, beheading, and maiming anyone that does not bow to their own personal version of Mohammad's demonic religion.

Allahu akbar—"Allah is the greatest"—is what a jihadist cries when he plunges a knife into someone, or decapitates them, or when, as a suicide bomber he triggers the bomb that will kill many and maim a multitude. Western politicians and the Western media evidently find no contradiction between Allah, whom they portray as God, and the barbaric acts that are carried out in Allah's name. This is because 99.99 percent of politicians and journalists are spiritually bankrupt and are, therefore, incapable of discerning the difference between chalk and cheese, between the followers of Allah and the followers of Jesus Christ, God's only begotten Son. Shame on them! They are the world's leaders and its spokespeople—they dupe millions.

15

The Hannibal Protocol

ISRAEL'S SECURITY CABINET MET for several hours in the evening of July 31 to discuss, among other things, a proposed 72-hour humanitarian ceasefire that had been jointly presented by the US and the UN. Hamas had accepted the ceasefire, which was to go into effect at 8:00 a.m. the following morning. Israel followed suit and also agreed. The agreement called for a complete halt to hostilities, but IDF forces could remain in Gaza and continue demolishing the Hamas attack tunnels. The UN was to monitor the Israeli troop lines to ensure there was no advance during the period of the ceasefire.

However, less than 90 minutes into the ceasefire Hamas gunmen sprang from a tunnel entrance behind a group of Israeli soldiers and attacked them, killing two IDF soldiers and mortally wounding another, Second-Lieutenant Hadar Goldin. Two gunmen, still firing machine guns, dragged Goldin down into the tunnel shaft. Other Israeli soldiers rushed to help Goldin and, disobeying explicit IDF commands, Eitan, the deputy commander of Goldin's Givati company, and who had been in combat with Goldin, entered the dangerous tunnel. As he clambered into the tunnel shaft he said to his men, "If I'm not out in five minutes I'm dead; just carry on." Risking his life, Eitan chased after the gunmen for several hundred meters (yards), but was unable to locate Goldin. He did, however, bring back sufficient equipment and evidence for the IDF forensic unit to establish that Goldin was dead, that he had not been kidnapped alive. Hamas has since acknowledged that it holds Goldin's remains and that their return hinges upon Israel accepting Hamas's demands for a longterm ceasefire. Israel did not give way to Hamas's immediate demands and Goldin's remains have not been returned five weeks following the ceasefire that went into effect on August 26, 2014.

When Second-Lieutenant Hadar Goldin was dragged into the tunnel one of the other soldiers shouted out loudly, "Hannibal!" After only a short interval all hell broke loose. Israel abandoned all restraints and heavily bombarded the area around the region of the attack upon the soldiers. The order was given, "If it moves, shoot." It was a desperate attempt to prevent the abducted soldier from being moved to another area. Israel's Hannibal Protocol had been implemented.

The Hannibal Protocol was drafted in the summer of 1986—one year after a lopsided agreement in which Israel traded 1,150 security prisoners in exchange for three Israeli soldiers, and some months after the abduction of two other soldiers, Yosef Fink and Rafael Alsheikh. The idea of the Hannibal Protocol was to establish a set procedure, known to every soldier, to limit the success of any abduction operation. Every IDF soldier, both male and female, must needs know that nothing will be spared in order to prevent a possible abduction by an enemy. At the same time, soldiers are also obligated to do everything in their power, even to the pulling of the pin on their own grenade, to prevent themselves from being abducted. Soldiers must make every effort to rescue another soldier or to prevent an abduction—short of actually killing the soldier themselves. The Hannibal Protocol gives every soldier clarity on the abduction issue.

The abduction of mortally wounded Hadar Goldin in Rafah triggered the use of the Hannibal procedure. The IDF used greatly increased firepower in an attempt to prevent Goldin falling into enemy hands. Over 100 Palestinians were killed in the intense Israeli air, land, and sea bombardment. It was yet another 100 Palestinian lives tossed away by Hamas which cares not a whit for Palestinian civilian blood. Israel was outraged by yet another Hamas violation of a humanitarian ceasefire, which this time included the abduction of a soldier.

The ceasefire fell apart completely and both Israel and Hamas intensified its fighting. At this point it was the seventh ceasefire in a row that Hamas had flouted; both the US administration and the UN laid the blame for the breakdown of the truce squarely on Hamas. The attack upon the Israeli soldiers came from under a house near the border town of Rafah. Hamas's account of the attack had several versions: One Hamas leader was quoted claiming responsibility for the soldier's capture, then backtracked. Other senior Hamas commanders contended that the attack took place at 7 a.m., before the ceasefire came into force even though Palestinian media reporting the fighting near Rafah began three hours later. One said that the Hamas gunmen had acted only to counter "Zionist incursions."

On Sunday, August 3, the IDF announced that Second-Lieutenant Hadar Goldin was officially dead and that a burial service was to be held for him. Goldin's death was confirmed by DNA testing of human remains recovered in a destroyed Hamas attack tunnel. Evidently, the incredibly fierce bombardment set in motion by the Hannibal procedure following Goldin's abduction had blown Goldin's body apart, along with those of his abductors. Israel was saddened by the confirmed death of Goldin, but was, at the same time, relieved that he was not in the hands of Hamas terrorists, which would have been a fate even worse than death.

Hamas itself called for a ceasefire and presented a list of demands in Cairo that it said had to be met if there was to be calm. If there was to be a ceasefire it would have to be "on our terms." The demands were:

1) Immediate IDF withdrawal from the Gaza Strip

2) Lifting of the blockade and opening of the border crossings

3) Extension of the fishing zone to 12 nautical miles

4) Lifting of the civilian no-go zone near the Gaza border fence

5) Creation of airport and seaport

6) Rehabilitation of the Gaza Strip through international donors

7) Release of the fourth batch of 32 prisoners from the failed talks between Israel and the PA in June when Abu Mazen's Palestinian Authority (PA) joined forces with the Hamas terror organization and created the "Unity Government."

8) Release of the prisoners set free in the Gilad Schalit deal and rearrested during Operation Brother's Keeper in the aftermath of the kidnapping and murder of the

three Israeli teenagers, and the release of Palestinian legislators.

Israeli officials dismissed this list of demands as "completely unrealistic." Israel informed Egypt that it would not be sending a delegation to Cairo to discuss a ceasefire because Hamas had broken all ceasefires thus far; therefore, negotiating another truce was simply a waste of time. Israel had made it clear time and time again that if Hamas stopped launching rockets into Israeli population centers then, and only then, would Israel cease firing. Israel's Prime Minister Binyamin Netanyahu also made it clear that there would be no withdrawal of Israeli troops from Gaza until all terror tunnels had been completely destroyed; however, on August 4 senior IDF officers indicated that almost all known tunnels had been destroyed. Israel's defense minister Moshe Ya'alon stressed that the campaign had not yet ended, but said it had "set Hamas back five years."

Hamas demands for the blockade of Gaza to be lifted and border crossings into Egypt and Israel opened were ludicrous demands insofar as Israel was concerned. If Hamas could amass around 10,000 short, medium, and long-range rockets as well as thousands of mortars while its land and sea borders were blockaded by Israel and Egypt in an attempt to prevent weapons and explosives entering Gaza, what can justifiably be expected if Gaza's borders were thrown wide open? The answer is obviously wholesale importation of weapons and explosives. Israeli leaders would have to be collectively insane to allow Gaza's borders to be opened while the Strip is still governed by Hamas. Only the demilitarization of Hamas, Islamic Jihad, et al, and reverting Gaza's government back to the PA could possibly allow for such a thing.

The above argument is also valid for not allowing Gaza to establish an airport and a seaport. Planeloads of weapons would arrive at such an airport and ships would arrive heavily laden with weapons at a seaport. Even in the current restricted fishing zone Gaza fishermen are involved in the bringing in of weapons and explosives; allowing their boats to go further from Gaza shores will only compound the problem. And releasing hundreds of Hamas operatives, along with previously convicted murderers of Israeli men, women, and children, will do nothing to foster peace between

Israel and the Palestinians. It is a documented fact that 68 percent of Palestinian prisoners released by Israel quickly return to terror activities. The no-go zone along the border with Gaza is to prevent Hamas from planting IEDs (Improvised Explosive Devices) along the border fence or penetrating the fence itself to carry out terror attacks in Israel.

Hamas demands that Gaza be rehabilitated by international donors, but the rehabilitation of Gaza must be linked to its de-militarization. Hamas spent 40 percent of its entire budget to build its terror tunnels and the manufacture of rockets to fire at Israeli civilian communities; donor countries did in fact fund the building of the underground terror city and the development of rockets. The international community needs to take a break from its vilifying of Israel over the damage and loss of life in Gaza and share responsibility for the rehabilitation of Gaza along with the demilitarizing of its terror organizations. Tut-tutting is not going to prevent further loss of Palestinian life in the future; only active boots-on-the-ground involvement can do that.

On August 2 the *Al-Hayat* newspaper reported that the European Union presented to Egypt a number of suggestions for lifting the blockade of the Gaza Strip. The EU reportedly suggested reopening the six crossings to and from the Gaza Strip to allow movement of people and goods. It also suggested that the Rafah crossing between Gaza and Egypt be manned by EU observers.

As it has been shown above, the opening of the border crossings is a non-starter for Israel while Hamas remains the governing power in Gaza; it is only jelly-brained talking heads that do not understand this reality. Under current conditions, such suggestions from the EU only proves its bankruptcy of sound ideas in the diplomatic arena in which it remains a dwarf. And the last time EU observers manned the Rafah crossing between Gaza and Egypt the observers ran from before Hamas like terrified children before a mythical dragon; they ran to the safety of an IDF base. They never returned to the Rafah crossing.

Israel is not about to place the safety of its nation and its people in the hands of the EU, the UN, or the US. The international community can step up to the plate and work alongside Israel to help bring peace and stability to this most volatile of regions, or it can sit back and do nothing but vilify Israel as has been its wont for several decades.

At this point there is a new 72-hour ceasefire brokered by Egypt in effect. Whether it holds or not is up to Hamas, no other ceasefire made it past the first hour or so without rockets being fired from Gaza into Israel. The ceasefire agreement is unconditional; Israel agreed to it because it believes its tunnel destruction is complete and at this stage has pulled all its troops out of Gaza; however, should rocket fire begin again the IAF will make further punishing strikes against Hamas targets.

The IDF believes it has destroyed all the terror attack tunnels that run underneath the Gaza-Israel border. This writer does not believe for one minute that the IDF has destroyed all the tunnels, but he has no wish to be proven correct by an infiltration of Hamas gunmen. This writer hopes and prays that Israel will quickly develop the technology by which tunnels can be detected even if they are constructed to a depth of a ten-story building below ground level as has been the reality in Gaza.

16

Mowing the grass

After 28 days of fighting an Egyptian-brokered 72-hour ceasefire came into effect at 8:00 a.m. on Tuesday, August 5; it was still holding, albeit it was wobbling a bit, on the morning of July 7. Egypt proposed the truce be extended by two days in order to allow further time for negotiating a more permanent ceasefire. Israel accepted Egypt's proposal, but Hamas rejected it, again. Hamas says it will resume the firing of rockets and mortars into Israel at 8:00 a.m. on Friday, July 8, unless its demands for a full and permanent opening of the Rafah crossing into Egypt and the release of Palestinian prisoners are met.

Hamas had, for the time being at least, dropped all of its other demands, which can only lead to the conclusion that it had suffered great losses and was clearly bested in this war that it had initiated; however, one of its gunmen will no doubt pop its head out of a hole and claim it won the war as is the Arab wont.

Hamas utilized the 72-hour reprieve from Israeli shelling and air strikes to reposition rocket launchers and gather together its remaining stocks of missiles. The terror organization cares not one whit about the 1,867 Gazans who have lost their lives in the fighting up until the time of this truce. Hamas leaders have remained hidden in a fortified bunker beneath Gaza's main hospital. Hamas leaders are prepared to once again initiate hostilities and to lose an infinite number of civilians, partly because it feels completely safe in its command center below the Shifa hospital, and partly because it still has an estimated 3,000 projectiles left in its arsenal; but primarily it is ready to initiate further catastrophic damage to Gaza because it sees that the weight of world opinion is heavily against Israel due to the devastation that has taken place in Gaza during the month-long war.

On August 6, after a month of fighting Israel, masked Hamas members gave *Al Jazeera*, the Qatar-based satellite news network, a look at how they have prepared for a new round of warfare following the end of the 72-hour ceasefire. Hamas showed *Al Jazeera* a tunnel that was still functioning and which was replete with rockets, mortars, anti-tank missiles, RPGs (Rocket Propelled Grenades), machine guns, etc. Hamas, they said, is sending a message to Israel that "our finger is still on the trigger." If our demands are not met, they said, our rockets are still ready to hit every area of Israel. That, however, is not negotiating; it is called blackmail.

Israel had pulled all its troops and armor out of Gaza and redeployed them along the Israeli side of its border with Gaza. Believing it had achieved its aim of destroying the threat presented by the vast terror tunnel city below Gaza—albeit at this point no one really believes the IDF has destroyed all the tunnels—and brought a drastic reduction in the number of rockets being fired, the IDF is now poised to forcefully respond should Hamas continue with its irrational missile belligerency. Only 25,000 of the 86,000 IDF reserve soldiers that were called up have been sent home since the guns fell silent on Tuesday, August 5; the remainder, together with all the armor and heavy guns, remained mobilized for war. The formal end of Operation Protective Edge is entirely dependent upon Hamas's actions after the ceasefire ends on Friday, August 8.

Egypt first presented a truce proposal that would have come into force on July 15, but Hamas rejected Egypt's peace overtures and opted to continue targeting Israeli population centers. Hamas said the ceasefire did not meet its demands. At that time, the death toll in Gaza was 197, and Israelis had only suffered a few injuries from fragments of rockets that were shot down by the Iron Dome missile defense system. Three weeks later, after being pummeled like never before, Hamas itself asked for a ceasefire. The current Egyptian ceasefire proposal contains the exact same conditions as the first proposal; the only difference now is that Gaza lies in ruins, 1,807 of it residents are now dead, along with 59 Israeli soldiers and four Israeli civilians. Only the mandatory bomb shelters and safe rooms in Israeli homes, businesses, cities, and towns prevented a catastrophe of cosmic proportions happening as a result of the 3,356 missiles that Hamas had fired into Israeli residential areas at this point. Obviously, the horrendous loss of life in Gaza must be left on the doorstep of Hamas; it had the opportunity to stop the fighting and negotiate a longer-term truce, but it spurned the chance, choosing instead to try and kill Jews with its ineffectual rockets and abortive attempts at terrorist infiltrations into Israel, which took the lives of 11 ambushed Israeli soldiers, but no civilian casualties.

Israel has confirmed that at this stage of the war it had killed an approximated 750 Hamas operatives and gunmen, destroyed 34 cross-border terror tunnels and somewhere around 3,000 rockets that were stored in weapons caches throughout northern Gaza. Hamas's stockpile of medium-range rockets, which it used to target Greater Tel Aviv and Jerusalem, had been depleted. Hamas had been firing far fewer of those rockets, apparently pacing itself for a longer, more drawn-out conflict. Of late, Hamas had focused on firing short-range rockets into southern Israeli towns and cities.

Israel demolished all of its Jewish communities that were in Gaza in August 2005; forcefully expelling some 9,000 Israelis from their homes where they had lived for more than 25 years. Israel bowed to international pressure from no-nothing humanist, Western politicians who said that if there was to be peace between Israel and the Palestinians Israel must withdraw from Gaza. Israel uprooted close to 9,000 of its citizens; pulling out of Gaza completely. Hamas moved in and created a terrorist Hamastan, which has fired over 18,000 rockets and mortars into Israel's southern border towns since Israel disengaged from Gaza in 2005.

In this third war with Hamas since 2005 it was never Israel's aim to reconquer the Gaza Strip. Its aim was to smash the tunnel network and destroy Hamas's ability to fire rockets into Israel. During the war it was established beyond argumentation that Hamas's Command Center was right under Shifa hospital, the main medical facility for Gaza's 1.7 million inhabitants. No matter what anyone says to the contrary, Israel has more than bent over backwards to reduce as much as possible the toll on civilians in this war, usually to its own detriment. The colossal damage inflicted upon Gaza is entirely due to Hamas and other terror groups firing their rockets from among densely populated areas, which Israel was forced to respond to. In the next post on this writer's blog he will include the URLs to which readers can go to and see Hamas's firings of rockets from among civilian areas. Such actions are classed as war crimes in the internationally recognized protocols of warfare.

It was only due to Israel's compassion for Gazan civilians that it did not bomb Shifa hospital in order to kill Hamas's top brass and explode the munitions that are stashed underneath the hospital. On Wednesday, August 6, Lieutenant-Colonel Ori Shechter, deputy commander of Israel's Nahal Brigade, said on *Army Radio*:

> Had the IDF been ordered to go and get the bunkered Hamas leaders, we would have gone to Shifa hospital and pulled them out by their ears.

According to Israel's *Channel 2* television, in the last week of July the IDF had presented to Israel's top ministers an assessment of what a full reconquest of Gaza would entail: To reestablish Israeli control over the Strip and clearing it of all military threats would involve the deaths of hundreds of soldiers and thousands of Palestinians. It would risk the kidnapping of soldiers, endanger Israel's peace treaties with Egypt and Jordan, batter Israel's economy, prompt riots and worse among the Israeli Arab community and in the West Bank—biblical Judea and Samaria—and take about five years. After the IDF briefing on reconquering Gaza, when Prime Minister Binyamin Netanyahu asked his minister colleagues if any of them wanted to pursue the idea, no one raised their hand. Israel would have to be content with occasionally "mowing the grass," the IDF term for its wars against Hamas.

17

That elusive ceasefire

ISRAEL ACCEPTED AN EGYPTIAN 72-hour cease-fire proposal late Monday night and it went into effect the next morning, August 5 at 8:00 a.m. It was Hamas that called for the time-out. It now appears that it was only a ploy in order to prepare for another round of fighting at the end of the truce. To Israel's surprise, the ceasefire was not violated by Hamas as were each of the seven previous ceasefires; it held for the full 72-hours. The quiet of the ceasefire was shattered by the first salvo of rockets out of Gaza, aimed at the Israeli city of Ashkelon. The time was 8:03 a.m.

Israel did not return fire; it held off in the hope that Hamas would see sense and stop firing; however, it was not to be. At 10:27 a.m., after 144 minutes of sustained rocket fire from Gaza, Prime Minister Binyamin Netanyahu and Defense Minister Moshe Ya'alon issued orders to the IDF to "respond with force." At 10:42 the IDF began air-strikes on Gaza targets and Israeli warships starting hitting more targets from the sea.

The aim of the three-day ceasefire was to allow Palestinian and Israeli delegations time to travel to Cairo and attempt to negotiate a longer term ceasefire. At 8:15 a.m. on Friday, Azzam al-Ahmad, the head of the Palestinian delegation to Cairo, told the media by telephone that Egypt had offered both sides another 72-hour truce, but that Hamas had refused.

An Egyptian security official said that in Cairo the Palestinian delegation's stance had hardened after the arrival of Hamas and Islamic Jihad leaders from Gaza. He said Azzam al-Ahmad, the leader of the Palestinian delegation and the representative of the PA President Abu Mazen, had threatened to withdraw from the talks if the two terror groups did not show more "flexibility." It was obvious that Hamas and Islamic Jihad were not in Cairo to negotiate a longterm ceasefire; they were there only to demand further conditions which they demanded be met if there was to be any extension of the 72-hour truce.

Israel refused Hamas's demand that the 54 Hamas operatives rearrested during the West Bank hunt for the killers of the three Israeli teenagers be released. The operatives had been released in a lopsided prisoner exchange in October 2011 when Israel released 1,027 prisoners for a single Israeli soldier who had been abducted five years earlier by Hamas. The soldier had been held in solitary confinement without seeing daylight or having any contact whatsoever with the Red Cross or the outside world during his years of captivity. The 54 prisoners which Israel rearrested during its June 2014 hunt for the murderers of the teenagers had all violated their terms of release and for that reason they were recaptured.

Hamas also demanded that the Rafah crossing into Egypt be opened permanently, and that international guarantees be provided that the crossing would never be closed again. However, it is not within Israel's jurisdiction to open the Rafah crossing. Israel had relinquished its authority over the Rafah crossing when it pulled out of Gaza in 2005; it handed the control of the crossing over to an EU observer force. But when Hamas took Gaza away from the PA by force in a bloody coup in June 2007 the EU observer force ran away and the jurisdiction for the opening of the crossing fell into the domain of Egypt. During the presidency of the Egyptian Muslim Brotherhood's Mohammed Morsi Rafah was open continuously and weapons flowed into Gaza (Hamas being an offshoot of Egypt's Muslim Brotherhood). However, when the Egyptian military, under the command of Abdel Fatah el-Sisi—now president of Egypt—removed Morsi from the presidency, the Rafah crossing was closed in order to prevent weapons being transported into Gaza. El-Sisi was no happier than Israel to have Islamic jihadists creating mayhem on its doorstep. In addition to keeping the Rafah crossing closed, except for emergency humanitarian purposes, el-Sisi ordered the destruction of the tunnels under the Gaza-Egypt border through which Hamas smuggled weapons, vehicles, fuel, cement, steel, etc. Hamas heavily taxed everything that entered the Strip through the tunnels and at this point the Egyptians have closed or destroyed 1,369 tunnels, which in effect severed Hamas's financial umbilical cord.

Quoting a "knowledgeable source," the Hamas daily *Al-Resalah* reported on August 7 that Egypt had informed the Palestinian delegation in Cairo that it had decided to exclude the Rafah crossing from negotiations. Egypt would only be willing to open the crossing following it being handed over to PA control.

An unsubstantiated rumor spread that Egypt kept the Palestinian delegation under house arrest while its members were in Cairo. As stated, that rumor was unsubstantiated; however, it is fact that a prominent Egyptian lawyer, Samir Sabri, called on Egypt's Attorney-General Hesham Barakat for those in the Hamas delegation to be handed over to investigators for criminal prosecution due to them being members of a terrorist group whose activities are banned in Egypt.

Unlike Egypt, Israel never closed its border crossings with Gaza during Operation Protective Edge. Even as mortar shells fell on the Erez crossing, used for pedestrian traffic, and the Kerem Shalom crossing, which is used for goods, trucks continued to enter the Gaza Strip and passengers continued to pass in and out of the territory. Since July 8, when the war began, until the 72-hour ceasefire, over 3,000 civilians crossed through Erez in both directions, nearly 1,000 of them for medical reasons. A total of 1,856 trucks, carrying 40,550 tons of aid was taken into Gaza—1,491 trucks with 37,178 tons of food, 220 trucks with 1,694 humanitarian supplies, and 106 trucks with 1,029 tons of medical supplies. These facts were hidden from the world by foreign journalists and broadcasters.

As mentioned above, Hamas did not go to Cairo to negotiate a ceasefire, it went only to make—as Israel's Minister of Justice Tzipi Livni termed it—"maximalist demands," which are impossible for Israel to accept. Hamas wants to continue ceasefire talks while it continued to fire rockets into Israel's towns and cities. Hamas does not negotiate, it simply demands, and its demands are the "take it or leave it" kind. Israel refuses to continue talks while Hamas and company keep up perpetual rocket barrages against Israeli civilians.

Hamas is pleased with itself because, as a Hamas spokesman said on August 7, it has "demonstrated an ability to surprise the enemy and cause it pain." And that is really all the twisted, evil mind of Hamas is aiming to do—cause Israelis pain. As this writer has said before, Hamas will fight to its last rocket and to the last drop of Palestinian civilian blood. Its masterminds are holed up in five-star hotels in Qatar, Turkey, London, Jordan, and Lebanon, enjoying the luxury that wealth brings, and its military leaders are bunkered down in impenetrable fortresses below ground. Ordinary Palestinians are barely existing amongst the horrendous rubble of Gaza; they survive in a depressing state of poverty. Defying all international attempts to broker a new truce, Hamas had vowed that it would make no concessions to Israel in ceasefire talks. Hamas had brought terrible suffering to the people of Gaza by its inhuman practice of storing its missiles in and firing them from schools, mosques, hospitals, and UN facilities.

This writer said in the last post that he would include URLs in the next post showing Hamas launching rockets from civilian areas in order for the reader to understand exactly what Israel is up against in its battle with its fanatical Islamic foe. However, including the substantial amount of information that is to hand from reporters in Gaza will make this current post far too long. This writer assures reader that he will include this information in the next post. That is assuming that Israel does not drop one of the bombs from its alleged nuclear arsenal on Hamas's command center beneath Shifa hospital like America did on Hiroshima in 1945—without notice.

18

Hypocritical journalism and artificial stupidity

THIS WRITER'S PREVIOUS POST stated that the 72-hour ceasefire between Israel and Hamas, which took effect on August 5 at 8:00 a.m., had, unlike the seven previous ceasefires that were all broken by Hamas, held for the full 72-hour term. This writer must here issue a correction of that information.

The quiet of the ceasefire was not broken by a salvo of rockets at 8:03 a.m. as the earlier post stated. Israeli officials have since confirmed that the ceasefire was broken by Hamas around 4:00 a.m. Evidently Hamas fired several rockets toward Israel's Eshkol region, and two more rockets in the closing minutes of the ceasefire, before the air was shattered at 8:03 a.m. by dozens of rockets being fired into Israel—including the salvo aimed at the city of Ashkelon.

At this present stage of the war there is another 72-hour ceasefire being observed by both Israel and Hamas; it went into effect at one minute past midnight on August 10. However, with either Hamas or one of its proxies breaking eight consecutive ceasefires thus far, what chance was there of the current ceasefire not being broken and the hostilities resumed? Hamas leaders had said the truce was the last chance for peace. There can be little doubt that Hamas's proclamation was intended to intimidate Israel and push it into yielding to Hamas's non-starter demands. What Hamas did not seem to realize was that rather than having pushed Israel into a corner, Israel was seriously considering launching a full-scale ground offensive against Hamas that would make the earlier one look like a picnic in comparison. A good few members of the Israeli Knesset, including some from the Security Cabinet, together with the great majority of the Israeli populace, wanted Israel to destroy the threat of Hamas rockets and terrorist infiltrations once and for all. This would only be possible through an Israeli invasion force that would go "all the way."

Prime Minister Binyamin Netanyahu is wary of a full-scale invasion of Gaza; he knows there will be heavy casualties among IDF soldiers and he does not want to have to live with that if it is at all avoidable. He wants quiet on Israel's southern border and he promised he would give the people that. Netanyahu is pragmatic; if there is a chance of obtaining peace and quiet for Israeli citizens without surrendering to Hamas's somewhat ludicrous demands he will work for that. Netanyahu is not a Neville Chamberlain or an Édouard Daladier, there would not be a "peace at any price" in order to bring "peace in our time." Netanyahu resisted ministerial pressure to decimate Hamas, but how long can he withstand the pressure? Netanyahu wants the international community to demilitarize Gaza and disarm all the terror groups, but no nation seems willing to get its hands dirty. When push comes to shove there are no cojones to be found among the nations that make up the international community.

If Netanyahu is out-voted in the security cabinet in a call for ousting Hamas militarily, he will have no option but to call up virtually the entire army and send it into Gaza. Numbers of soldiers who fought in Gaza during the recent ground offensive have, in contravention of IDF orders, expressed their disappointment at not having been allowed to continue the offensive until Hamas was unable to rise from the dust; they say they are ready to risk their lives to bring peace to their country. And Israelis, cognizant of the fact that they may well lose sons, husbands, brothers, and friends, have weighed the pros and cons and are willing to suffer the loss sooner rather than later when the threat from Gaza will be much, much worse.

In the last post it was mentioned that 40,550 tons of aid—some 1,500 truckloads of food, medicines, and humanitarian aids—were sent into Gaza from Israel during the war with Hamas. However, the Kerem Shalom border crossing, through which the trucks carrying the aid pass from Israel to Gaza, was targeted on several occasions by mortar attacks just prior to the current ceasefire coming into effect. Several mortars landed inside the crossing causing extensive damage and trucks carrying highly inflammable fuel and oil narrowly escaped being turned into fire-balls. At this point the crossing is closed to assess the damage.

The members of Hamas and its terrorist proxies possess not one single humanitarian cell between them. They use the old, the weak and feeble, the women, and the children of Gaza as human shields in order to get the casualty numbers up. Civilians are used as mere public relations fodder. And now, just before the latest truce went into effect, Hamas deliberately targets the sole crossing through which humanitarian aid can enter, and which only relieves a little of the dreadful distress in which the miserable civilians have found themselves in. And yet, unbelievably, almost the entire Western world is in an uproar over the ill-perceived inhumanity of Israeli forces that have had the courage to hit back at Gaza's terrorist minions who are endeavoring to snuff out all human life in Israel. This unmitigated stupidity is generated by overt anti-Semitism, which is partly due to the policies of myopic Western politicians who threw open their nation's gates and welcomed millions of Jew-hating Islamists into their midst.

The apocalyptic destruction in Gaza that we have all witnessed via our television screens is due to Hamas's orders to journalists; they are to show only building damage and bodies, especially bodies of children. If journalists defied Hamas's orders they were not allowed to broadcast and were restricted to their hotels. Almost all journalists who reported from Gaza refused, even on condition of anonymity, to speak to the Israeli media about the intimidation they were subjected to by Hamas. They were in fear of Hamas retaliation and happily toed the Hamas line in their reporting. This meant they deliberately concentrated on showing the colossal amount of damage that had befallen Gaza and both showed and talked about the number of dead "innocent civilians." As instructed by Hamas the journalists and broadcasters concentrated on showing bodies of women and children—the result of "Israeli aggression." Most journalists were also sure to mention Israel's "disproportionate" responses to Palestinian rocket fire, which almost no reporter seemed to have ever witnessed during his or her time in Gaza covering a war in which close to 4,700 rockets had been launched into Israel. This is nothing less than artificial stupidity, almost as ridiculous as the folk who take the reporting from Gaza to be the gospel truth.

According to Israel's Government Press Office, some 705 journalists from 42 countries came to Israel specifically to cover the Gaza conflict. This number joined the 750 journalists who are permanently stationed in Israel. With the world being so anti-Israel in the best of times the Jewish state is always a hot news item no matter what it does. Jerusalem's foreign press office is the third largest in the world, only Washington and Moscow permanently host more foreign journalists than Jerusalem. Israel is placed under a microscope and is held to a standard higher than any other nation. Even the UN Human Rights Council has Israel slotted into its agenda for every single meeting, something no other nation in the world is subjected to. Hypocrisy and anti-Semitism is very much alive and flourishing in the UN world, the media world, and the Western world in general.

A Press Office statement said that during the coverage of the Israel-Hamas fighting journalists often received threats and—in several cases—were the victims of violence that included destruction of their equipment. This was due to them having documented criminal activity by Hamas such as the launching of rockets from the heart of civilian areas. Several Western journalists in Gaza had been harassed and threatened by Hamas for documenting cases of the terrorist group's involvement of civilians in warfare. The *Times of Israel* confirmed several incidents in which journalists were questioned and threatened. These included cases involving photographers who had taken pictures of Hamas operatives in compromising circumstances—gunmen preparing to shoot rockets from within civilian structures, and/or fighting in civilian clothing—and who were then approached by Hamas men, bullied and had their equipment taken away.

One or two journalists said there was no intimidation by Hamas, but it is patently obvious that they only said this because they had not the courage to admit that due to Hamas's intimidation they were themselves guilty of fudging the facts in their biased reports from Gaza. The overwhelming majority of journalists and broadcasters that reported on the recent Gaza war blatantly ignored T. E. Utley's unwritten rules of journalism, the first of which is to report "accurately" and with "fanatical detachment." Instead, they falsified facts by simply omitting them; and when this writer studied law in bygone years a party was "guilty of fraud by deception through the omission of facts that are known to him." Therefore, the journalists that toed the Hamas line were guilty of fraud by deception, simply by omitting facts known to be true, which could have entirely changed the perception of the war being waged by Israel against Hamas. Clearly, the great majority of journalists reporting from Gaza controlled the minds and hearts of viewers and readers by omitting facts that could have influenced the perception of events as they unfolded. Instead, the viewers and listeners were fed a pre-packaged, pre-digested diet of poor Palestinian, nasty Israeli meals. Some of the journalists were at war with Israel themselves.

But one journalist, Christian Stephen, founder of Freelance Society, a media company specializing in hostile environments and conflict zones, agreed to discuss his experience while reporting from Gaza because he was heading to Iraq. Stephen quipped, "Hamas can't get me there."

Asked by the *Jerusalem Post* if he had photographs he could show Stephen said:

> Unfortunately, I don't have any shots for you. I saw a good amount of buildings releasing rocket fire towards Israel; however, the fighters were more or less ghosts in living rooms.

He told the English-language *Post*, "Gazans only want us to show damage, not shooting." He was brutally honest when he said:

> Any journalist who professes to observe without bias, feeling or fear is a liar, as well as any journalist who claims they are without apprehension of the consequences when working in a geographic raw nerve.

Without doubt the coverage of the war with Gaza has been heavily biased against Israel and the images presented day after day have totally misrepresented what the war was about. It was an insidious double standard and an example of true media duplicity. Few and far between have been the journalists who have stood with Israel by reporting fairly. Sean Hannity of *Fox News* was one of those people and he deserved an award for his integrity. Apart from most Israeli journalists and two or three others, Hannity stood alone.

However, a few journalists did run the gauntlet in Gaza when they either tweeted or reported on rocket fire from civilian areas. A television reporter from the Finnish *Helsingin Sanomat* confirmed on August 1 that Hamas had been firing rockets out of the Shifa Hospital, the main Gaza medical facility. The reporter, who was not named for security reasons, said that a rocket was launched "right in the back the parking lot" of the hospital at 2 a.m. on Friday morning. "Really, it happened right in the area, the sound of it was really loud," she said, adding, "It's true that rockets are launched here from the Gazan side into Israel."

In a denunciatory August 10 critique in *Tablet* of the international coverage of the Israeli-Hamas conflict, Matti Friedman, a former reporter and editor at the *Associated Press's* (*AP's*) Jerusalem bureau from 2006 to the end of 2011, gave some revelations about the journalistic attitudes behind *AP's* coverage of the Israeli-Palestinian conflict. Friedman explained that "the agency is wholly average" among large international peddlers of news that purportedly cover the conflict with "impartiality." Regarding Hamas's attempts to intimidate reporters Friedman said:

> Any veteran of the press corps here knows the intimidation is real. During the 2008–2009 Gaza fighting I personally erased a key detail—that Hamas fighters were dressed as civilians and being counted as civilians in the death toll.

Friedman adds to that: "The policy was then, and remains, not to inform readers that the story is censored unless the censorship is Israeli." He then goes on to say:

> Most reporters in Gaza believe their job is to document violence directed by Israel at Palestinian civilians. That is the essence of the Israel story. Facts only muddy the simple story they have been sent to tell.

Friedman also charged that, "Anything that doesn't fit the preordained story doesn't get published" and that *AP's* narrative was that "the Palestinians were moderate and the Israelis recalcitrant and increasingly extreme." Friedman ended by saying:

> Many of the people deciding what you will read and see view their role not as explanatory, but as political. Coverage is a weapon to be placed at the disposal of the side they like.

So, there we have it from the horse's mouth!

In an August 26 talk in Jerusalem at the Israel Center, Dr. Richard Landes, the director and co-founder of the Center of Millennial Studies at Boston University, said that "Western news organizations have failed to see and understand Hamas's media strategy as part of the global jihad war." Landes coined the phrase "Pallywood" in describing Palestinian obfuscation and outright lying in reporting news events and he sees a brand of "advocacy journalism" unfolding in the Israel-Palestinian conflict. Landes cited a *BBC* reporter who announced in 2001 at a Hamas rally, "We journalists stand shoulder to shoulder with you in your struggle against Israel."

In an August 10 rebuke of Gaza's de facto rulers that was posted on its website, the *Foreign Press Association* (*FPA*) denounced Hamas for controlling foreign press coverage and its discrimination against those who did not comply with its demands. In its statement the *FPA* said:

> The *FPA* protests in the strongest terms the blatant, incessant, forceful and unorthodox methods employed by the Hamas authorities and their representatives against visiting international journalists in Gaza over the past month.

The *FPA* asserted that:

> [I]n several cases, foreign reporters working in Gaza have been harassed, threatened or questioned over stories or information they have reported through their news media or by means of social media.

A number of reporters working in Gaza reported on Hamas's use of civilian infrastructure for military means, but said they were only able to do so once out of the Strip, for fear of Hamas reprisals.

Hamas itself admitted that it harassed journalists because those who reported on missile firings from civilian areas were guilty of "collaborating with the enemy."

Hamas spokeswoman, Isra Al-Mudallal, told the Lebanese TV station *Mayadeen TV* in an interview via *Skype* on August 15 that journalists who filmed "places from where missiles were launched" were "forced" by security personnel to stop. "These journalists were deported from the Gaza Strip; the security agencies would go and have a chat with these people." She explained that Hamas security personnel would give the journalists "some time to change their message" and "one way or another" they would be "forced" to change their reporting.

Regarding Gaza's Shifa hospital, an Israeli official said:

> We know that downstairs there is a Hamas command and control center and that Hamas leaders are hiding there. No reporter is allowed to go anywhere downstairs. They're only allowed to work upstairs to take pictures of casualties, the pictures that Hamas wants them to take.

The *Washington Post* reported on July 15 that Shifa had indeed "become a de facto headquarters for Hamas leaders, who can be seen in the hallways and offices."

A reporter in the Gaza Strip had her live broadcast interrupted when a rocket launched by Hamas whistled past over her head, startling her. The launch site was in such close proximity that the area was immediately lit up by the launching. Speaking in Arabic, the reporter informs her audience about the civilian casualties and even mentions the dangers posed to journalists before the very area she was reporting was thrust into the war-zone.

The extensive use of civilian areas and infrastructure had posed a continuing challenge to the IDF, which must respond to enemy fire from those areas. On August 4 India's *NDTV* filmed what the *New York Times* said it could not: footage of Hamas fighters in Gaza assembling and then launching a rocket aimed at Israel, from a residential area. The launch took place in a dense, urban environment in Gaza with plenty of civilians around — and one intrepid Indian reporter, Sreenivasan Jain. The report by Jain on

India's *NDTV* shows a Palestinian rocket crew using a tent as cover to set up a rocket launch, then launching the rocket. Jain notes that the Hamas rocket launch takes places "meters away from our hotel" and "bang in the middle of what is a residential area full of hotels and apartment buildings." Jain then heads to the spot from where the rocket was fired, but is "asked by people not to go to the location, so we're just pulling back..." Readers can copy the URL below into their internet browsers and watch the video:

http://www.timesofisrael.com/indian-tv-shows-hamas-rocket-fired-near-gaza-hotel/

In the text that accompanied the video report on *NDTV's* website, Jain wrote that it was published

> after our team left the Gaza Strip—Hamas has not taken very kindly to any reporting of its rockets being fired. But just as we reported the devastating consequences of Israel's offensive on Gaza's civilians, it is equally important to report on how Hamas places those very civilians at risk by firing rockets deep from the heart of civilian zones.

Two days later, Jain published an article on *NDTV's* website with the story behind his report, explaining that his team waited days before airing the video clip due to

> fear of reprisals from Hamas against us and those who worked with us, fear of inviting an Israeli response on the spot.

In a previous blog this writer criticized *France24* reporter Gallagher Fenwick for conforming to the Hamas story-line to show only damage and bodies; however, while Fenwick was giving his usual Hamas-scripted version of events on August 5 a rocket was fired from close to where he was reporting from and that apparently was too close for comfort and caused Fenwick to change his tune; the brief, shocked look on his face is priceless. The French TV station, *France24*, also showed a rocket launching pad, located about 100 yards (meters) from a UN building flying the blue UN flag. A hotel housing journalists covering the Gaza conflict was located about 50 meters (yards) from the launching pad, according to Fenwick who was reporting from Gaza City. Fenwick and members of his crew were forced to take cover when reporting from the site when the rocket was unexpectedly launched from nearby. Fenwick reported factually for a change:

> This type of setup is at the heart of the debate. The Israeli army has repeatedly accused the Palestinian militants of shooting from within densely populated civilian areas and that is precisely the type of setup we have here.

The URL is given below; interested readers can copy it into their internet browsers:

> http://www.france24.com/en/20140805-exclusive-video-hamas-rocket-launching-pad-near-gaza-homes-un-building/

On Wednesday, August 6, the *Christian Broadcasting Network* (*CBN*) aired an interview with Archbishop Alexios, whom reporter George Thomas called "Gaza's most prominent Christian leader." *CBN* estimates there are some 1,500 Christians living in Gaza. Alexios said Hamas used Gaza City's Greek Orthodox church compound to fire rockets at Israeli communities, but he would not discuss details on camera for security reasons.

When the IDF expanded its offensive in the Gaza enclave in July, Archbishop Alexios of the Saint Porphyrios church made the decision to open the site's doors in a show of interfaith solidarity, offering food, drink, and shelter to around 2,000 Gazans, regardless of their religion. A frightened Alexios claimed that even with Palestinians crowding the church, Islamist fighters had set up a rocket launching site in the compound. The URL to the video is too long to reproduce here at 419 characters; however, interested readers can Google it.

Many Israelis are frustrated at how badly the Gaza conflict had been reported and understood overseas. With the exception of the occasional courageous Finn and unflinching Indian, none of the hordes of super-professional journalists in Gaza could document the almost 5,000 rocket launches—including over 600 from near schools and other civilian facilities? Only four out of several hundred journalists saw Hamas gunmen firing from homes and hospitals? Only two out of hundreds saw Hamas gunmen dressed in civilian clothes? As this writer said earlier, anti-Semitism is alive and flourishing in the media world.

Melanie Phillips, the British journalist, author, and commentator was voicing her obvious disgust at the media coverage emanating from Gaza during an August 10 interview on Israel's *Channel 10* television. Phillips suggested that Israel ban journalists from reporting from Gaza, but, she added, "I don't know how you can do that."

Melanie Phillips was patently on Israel's side insofar as the reporting of the Gaza war was concerned, but on the other side, aligned to the anti-Israel hordes, we have a mustachioed zero, Geraldo Rivera, who holds himself to be some sort of expert on conflicts, but who in reality knows only a little more about conflicts than the man in the moon does. Rivera appeared on *Fox News* and castigated Israel for its actions in Gaza; he was not merely blasting Israel, he was downright ugly. This writer always wondered why he did not like Rivera, but after seeing and hearing him on *Fox Five* he knew why: he is a self-opinionated, pompous, anti-Semitic fraud. Rivera let forth about how he had covered conflicts for decades and that Israel hit a UNRWA school with a tank shell which is only accurate within two football fields and that it should use Hellfire missiles, blah, blah, blah. However, Rivera was quoting almost verbatim what a UN military man in Gaza had said two days earlier, right down to the UN man's ifs and buts. It was good to see that the girls on *Fox Five* jumped on Rivera and took him to task for his very obvious aversion to Israel. In this writer's opinion Geraldo Rivera is nothing but a bag of hot air with an overgrown mustache. This writer and his wife changed channels; we could not stomach more of Rivera.

WND's Thomas Sowell, referring to Rivera's criticism of Matt Drudge, wondered whether we are not in a "post-thinking era." He called Rivera's criticism "artificial stupidity." And that about sums up Geraldo Rivera and all the other anti-Semitic leftists who pose as journalists, but who are really nothing less than propagandists for the growing anti-Israel bloc. Shame on you all!

19

All's fair in love and war? (1)

THE TWELFTH AND LAST ceasefire was again broken by Hamas a full eight hours before it was due to expire at midnight on August 19. Israel immediately withdrew its delegation from the ceasefire talks in Egypt as it refused to negotiate under fire. A Hamas official, a member of the Palestinian delegation in Cairo, blamed Israel for the breakdown in truce talks and postulated: "Israel imposed war on us again." Israel responded to the renewed rocket fire with airstrikes against Hamas and other terrorist targets; and since the resumption of hostilities on August 20 IAF strikes have inflicted terrible damage to both the Hamas leadership and also upon its infrastructure in Gaza.

Israel's "most wanted" Hamas operative, Muhammad Deif, was also targeted in the early hours of the morning of August 20 when the IAF dropped two bunker-buster bombs on his home, killing Deif's wife, son, and daughter; there has been no confirmation that Deif was actually killed in the strike. Hamas says that Deif was not at home that night; that he is still alive and operating as Hamas's military chief; however, it has offered no proof to substantiate its claim that he is alive. Israel believes Deif died in the attack and that Hamas was bluffing in an attempt to cover up a very significant military loss as well as huge losses of face and public support. A photograph of a Shifa hospital death certificate released hours after the air-strike gave the names of Deif's wife and son; however, later that morning another certificate was released that showed the name of Muhammad Deif as well as his wife and son. This begs the question of which one is the true certificate? Did Deif die or did he survive?

Deif has had the survival rate of a cat. He survived four previous assassination attempts and from all those strikes against him he suffered the loss of his legs, his arms, and one eye, yet he continued to command the al-Qassam Martyrs Brigades—the armed wing of Hamas—and is responsible for the planning and overseeing of the attacks against Israel. For the most part Deif has lived furtively in hiding—out of sight for years—rarely even going to his home; however, Israel says that it would not have targeted Deif's home if it did not have strong intelligence that he was there.

The following day Lebanese media reported that Hamas's political kingpin, Khaled Mashaal, who is cloistered in a five-star hotel in Qatar, was being pressured to agree to an Egyptian ceasefire proposal. Mashaal wished to consult directly with Muhammad Deif and did so contrary to all established Hamas secrecy protocols. Mashaal broke official procedure and directly contacted Deif in the Gaza Strip to discuss a ceasefire with Israel, a call that was evidently intercepted by Israeli intelligence and which pinpointed Deif's location. The Lebanese report stated that shortly after the contact Israel authorized an air-strike on Deif's Gaza City residence.

The debatable question of whether Muhammad Deif was or was not killed by Israel in its fifth attempt on his life was soon bulldozed off the Israeli news headlines. A report that three top Hamas commanders had been killed in a single Israeli air-strike was cause for celebration in Israel. The three senior commanders—Muhammed Abu Shamaleh, Muhammed Barhoum and Raed al-Attar—were killed in an air-strike as they met in a home near the southern Gazan town of Rafah early in the morning on August 21. Israel said that Hamas's military wing has few commanders, and that the assassinations would be a heavy blow to the terror organization.

Hamas was indeed stunned. Its leaders were left in a state of shock. In a knee-jerk reaction Hamas began arresting Palestinian men, accusing them of being Israeli collaborators, and summarily executing them. Numbers of Palestinians had been previously executed under the pretext of their being collaborators with Israel; it has always been a convenient charge and an apparent acceptable way to cover up Hamas murders. However, following the deadly air-strike on the three commanders Hamas gunmen threw themselves into frenzied overdrive, publicly executing seven Palestinians the same day as the air-strike.

A further 18 Palestinians were executed the following day; six of those were dragged out of a crowd of worshipers exiting a mosque, thrown to the ground and riddled with bullets. Others were lined up against a wall and sprayed with bullets. Over the next days more Palestinians were killed after being accused of having "collaborated" with Israel. At the height of Israel's Operation Protective Edge a Palestinian media source said that 30 suspected collaborators had been executed, which at that point brought the total of known executions of "suspected collaborators" to 42 since the beginning of the latest round of hostilities.

Israel obviously uses human intelligence, which is known in intelligence circles as HUMINT; however, it is highly unlikely that Israel could manage to field anywhere near 42 Gazans cooperating in spying against Hamas when there is such an atmosphere of fear and terror in Gaza. Many Gazan men have been shot in their knees for simply being a member of Abu Mazen's Fatah faction and not a member of Hamas. A number of Fatah members were also thrown down to their death from the tops of high-rise buildings. A good number of high-ranking Fatah officials were placed under house arrest by Hamas and were made to endure the Israeli bombs and missiles; those attempting to leave their prison houses were shot in the legs by Hamas gunmen.

The Hamas terror group is paranoid about information being passed over to Israel or anyone else. This fact was acutely demonstrated by its execution of its own Hamas official Ayman Taha two weeks ago (first week of August) over suspicions that he collaborated with an Arab intelligence agency. In reality, Hamas gunmen live only to kill and maim, and it appears that the recent spate of bloody executions was motivated by sheer panic on the part of Hamas. It was initially reported that Taha's battered body was pulled from a collapsed building in the Shejaiya neighborhood following an Israeli air-strike and transferred to Shifa hospital. At Shifa it was found that Taha had been shot several times in the head and chest, the result of a Hamas firing squad; however, Taha was included in the "innocent civilian" casualty list of those killed by Israel.

Hamas cannot understand how Israel knows what it obviously knows. And Israel uses its intelligence to deadly effect. Another Hamas official was targeted by the IAF on Sunday, August 24.

The air force struck Muhammad Al-Aoul, a top figure in Hamas's finance division, making him the latest high-ranking member of the terror organization to be targeted in recent days. Apparently, bundles of money were scattered round about Al-Aoul's wrecked car, which could only mean money was still flowing into Gaza via yet undiscovered tunnels beneath the border with Egypt.

Deadly air-strikes were taking place on a daily basis, which without doubt meant that Israel's intelligence network suffered no loss from the wholesale slaughter of so-called "Israeli collaborators." Israel's intelligence service was aware of the names of those executed and none had links to Israel apart from one or two who had relatives living within Israel's Green Line. The poor folk that got executed were Palestinians unfortunate enough to catch the eye of Hamas gunmen who swiftly dispatched them to hell, adding them to all the other hundreds of "innocent civilians" whom Israel is said to have killed.

Hamas has yet to learn that God Almighty chose to give the average Jewish person a higher intelligence than the average Gentile person. That statement is not racist or elitist, it is the truth: In Exodus 4:22 Almighty God says: *"Israel is My son, My firstborn,"* and in Deuteronomy 21:17 God says that the *"firstborn son"* shall receive *"a double portion"* of all that the father has, *"it is the right of the firstborn,"* thus Israel, as God's firstborn son, has received a double portion, which includes intelligence, and this is borne out by the simple fact that Jews have received one third of all the Nobel prizes, even though Jews only constitute one half of one percent of the world's population. Israel's capabilities in the intelligence and high-tech fields is legendary. Hamas was finding this out the hard way.

20

All's fair in love and war? (2)

THE BREAKING OF THE ceasefire that instigated the latest round of rocket firings into Israel, and the consequential devastating responsive air-strikes by the IAF on Hamas targets in Gaza, may well have been a deliberate act ordered by Hamas's chief honcho Khaled Mashaal in Qatar. An analysis of events does indicate that Mashaal was under extreme pressure to reject an Egyptian truce proposal that would have taken effect immediately upon the heels of the then current ceasefire. Mashaal could well have ordered a major violation of the ceasefire in order to scuttle a further Egyptian ceasefire, knowing full well that Israel adamantly refuses to negotiate under fire.

Hamas wanted its allies and financial backers, Qatar and Turkey, to negotiate a truce with Israel on its behalf. America was also endeavoring to negotiate an agreement with the help of Qatar and Turkey; any such agreement would have contained virtually every Hamas demand. Israel, however, was having none of it. Israel knew full well that Qatar had poured hundreds of millions of dollars into establishing Hamas as the preeminent power in Gaza and had, therefore, provided the wherewithal for Hamas to amass its weapons arsenal and build its underground terror-tunnel city. Egypt felt that most of Hamas's demands were too extreme and did not even include them for discussion in the indirect talks with Israel. Hamas said that there would be no peace unless all their demands were met. Israel, on the other hand, could not allow Hamas to have what it demanded and preferred that there be no agreement. No agreement, it argued, was better than a bad agreement.

Israel's core demand was that Hamas be disarmed and the Gaza Strip be demilitarized. Hamas, however, refuses to entertain disarmament and threatens to kill anyone who tries to take its weapons. The international community does not have the cojones that are necessary to forcefully demilitarize Gaza; it is happy to continue lambasting Israel for using what it perceives to be "disproportionate" force when wars break out. When jihadism makes its way into Europe, as it eventually will, and begins to fire rockets into European cities or to kill and decapitate its citizens as ISIS is doing in Iraq and Syria, there may, just may, be a change in Europe's attitude toward Israel and toward Islamic savagery.

Egypt holds no love for Hamas due to it being an offshoot of the Egyptian Muslim Brotherhood, which is both classified as a terrorist organization in Egypt and also banned from pursuing any activities. Hamas has been involved in numerous terrorist attacks against Egyptian security forces, therefore Egypt is not about to give Hamas free reign in any ceasefire agreement with Israel that would allow it to bring in weapons via the Rafah crossing, which Egypt controls. The permanent opening of the Rafah crossing is a key Hamas demand for any ceasefire agreement. However, Egypt is the only viable ceasefire broker insofar as Israel is concerned and Hamas was being pressured to sign an Egyptian-brokered ceasefire agreement that only slightly begins to address Hamas demands. Egypt will only allow the Rafah crossing, between Gaza and Egypt, to be opened under the supervision of Abu Mazen's— only Westerners refer to Abu Mazen as Mahmoud Abbas—Fatah security forces, which sidelines Hamas entirely. If Hamas wants to break the siege of Gaza via the opening of the Rafah crossing, it has to eat crow and accept the Egyptian proposal.

Hamas had declared time and again that there would be no more ceasefires with Israel; however, it had taken such a beating from Israeli air-strikes and from the demolition of dozens of its terror tunnels, that it found itself between a rock and a hard place. It will eventually be forced to accept an Egyptian-brokered ceasefire agreement; it must cave in due to the catastrophic destruction that has been unleashed upon Gaza. Apparently, Hamas was about to wave a white flag before it broke the last ceasefire and by so doing it opened the gates of hell upon itself.

A truce would have come into effect long before had it not been for Hamas's kingpin Khaled Mashaal. He has been the central force that has prevented a long-term ceasefire between Israel and the Palestinian terror groups; he torpedoed every deal. Mashaal is ensconced abroad in a five-star Qatar hotel and is enmeshed in a disagreement with the local Hamas leadership in Gaza. In Gaza, Hamas watched and felt the pain as Israel systematically demolished everything Hamas held dear, but that did not touch Mashaal in Qatar. Saeb Erekat, Abu Mazen's right-hand man, delivered a message from the Palestinian president asking Mashaal to support the Egyptian ceasefire proposal. Erekat said that a truce with Israel should be consolidated. Speaking to Palestinian leaders on August 23 Abu Mazen said there was no alternative to the Egyptian initiative for a long-term truce.

Senior Israeli officials said Israel has information that Khaled Mashaal acted to sabotage the ceasefire in order to undermine the Egyptian initiative. Mashaal's goal, they said, was to advance the Qatar-Turkey proposal that greatly differed from the one put forward by Egypt.

Qatar understood that Mashaal was under pressure to accept the Egyptian proposal and that he was about to throw in the towel and accept. A report by *al-Hayat*, the London-based Arab daily, said that a high-ranking official in Abu Mazen's Fatah faction says Qatar threatened to expel Mashaal if he agreed to the Egyptian proposal for a ceasefire in its current format. Qatar also wanted a Qatari representative to be invited to Cairo to participate in the talks.

It is this writer's belief that Mashaal ordered the then ceasefire to be broken in order to sink the proposal being put forward by Egypt. Mashaal's apparent thinking was that it was more pragmatic for Gaza to lose more structures and more civilians than for him to be expelled from Qatar; torn from his life of wealth and grandeur. Such bravery, such courage, such valor! He remains the same cringing terrorist that he has always been—hiding himself away in five-star hotels while his underlings are killed and their command centers razed. Syria expelled Mashaal, but the emir of the oil-rich mini-kingdom of Qatar picked up Mashaal's tab and keeps him in the style he has become accustomed to.

Qatar funds Islamic terrorism and terrorists everywhere, but it has a special relationship with Hamas and liberally finances it. In an August 25 *New York Times* opinion piece, Israel's Ambassador to the UN Ron Prosor calls on the international community to stop

Qatar's funding of Hamas activities. Prosor called Qatar the "Club Med for Terrorists" and wrote in his op-ed:

> Today, the petite petroleum kingdom is determined to buy its way to regional hegemony, and like other actors in the Middle East, it has used proxies to leverage influence and destabilize rivals. Every one of Hamas's tunnels and rockets might as well have had a sign that read 'Made possible through a kind donation from the emir of Qatar.'

On August 26 the Israeli media had a number of articles quoting Hamas and Palestinian Islamic Jihad being in favor of an immediate truce. In comments made to the Arabic daily *Al-Hayat*, senior Hamas official, spokesman and political bureau number-two (after Khaled Mashaal) Moussa Abu Marzouk, says Hamas accepts the formulation in the latest Egyptian ceasefire proposal. An Islamic Jihad official told *Al-Hayat* that the Egyptian proposal will strengthen the PA in Gaza, as it gives the West Bank-based authority control of Gaza's border crossings—a proposal already accepted by members of Israel's security cabinet.

The Islamic Jihad official said his group decided to accept the Egyptian proposal in order to "prevent the deaths of more Palestinian children." He added that Israel failed in Operation Protective Edge because "it has failed to disarm the Gaza Strip or prevent the construction of additional tunnels."

We see from the last statement an overt endeavor to save face, which is very important to Arabs. Israel has devastated the Hamas and Islamic Jihad infrastructures and also killed many hundreds of their operatives and gunmen. Thousands of buildings, up to 15 stories high, have been leveled to the ground because embedded in them were terrorist command centers. There is considerable damage done to homes in Israel as a result of the actual count of 4,564 rockets that were fired into Israeli populated areas, but only seven civilians, including a four-year-old child, died as a result. Israel's Iron Dome missile defense system intercepted 735 rockets heading for the nation's most heavily populated areas.

Israel also mourned the loss of 65 of its soldiers who gave their lives defending their country. During the latest round of hostilities both Hamas and Islamic Jihad have repeatedly claimed to have won the war—as they have done throughout and at the end of every war—and Hamas loudly and proudly made the claim again, this time with street celebrations and gunfire, on August 26 when an open-ended ceasefire was announced. *France24* gave full and repeated coverage to Hamas's claim to have won the war by having beaten Israel.

"We have won," Hamas spokesman Sami Abu Zuhri ecstatically proclaimed at a news conference in front of Shifa Hospital. He said the group's fighters had accomplished "what no Arab army has done. We have defeated them," referring to Israel. Hamas's big deal of claiming victory over Israel should be placed into perspective: the ceasefire it claims to have successfully "negotiated" is the exact same proposal that Egypt offered on July 15, one week following the outbreak of the war. Israel accepted the ceasefire proposal at that time, but Hamas spurned it. On August 26 Hamas was loudly celebrating its negotiation of a ceasefire that fulfilled its demands when in fact there is absolutely nothing more to the proposal than there was a month and a half ago. Israel lost nothing by agreeing to the ceasefire and Hamas gained nothing from accepting it.

In the end, Hamas was forced to eat crow. Besides the destruction of its military infrastructure it had lost 40 of its senior commanders and Islamic Jihad had lost ten of theirs; both Hamas and Islamic Jihad had been represented at the Cairo ceasefire talks and both had come home with nothing to show for their weeks-long rocket and mortar offensive against Israel. On the afternoon of August 26, when first word of the ceasefire began to emerge, it became abundantly clear that Hamas had capitulated, retreated with its tail between its legs; it had abandoned everything it had insisted upon.

On September 30 the *Times of Israel* reported that on September 28 former OC Southern Command, Major-General (res.) Tal Russo spoke at The Institute for Policy and Strategy in Herzliya. Russo apparently said that Israel had made "no shortage" of mistakes regarding the attack tunnel threat prior to Operation Protective Edge, but went on to say that even so Hamas was still pulling bodies out of the destroyed tunnels and there is "a stench of death" hanging over the area. Russo also said that Israel should not concern itself too much about finding the perfect technological solution for detecting all underground digging, but rather it should concentrate on how to turn the tunnels "into death traps." The following day, at Jerusalem's Bar Ilan University, Defense Minister Moshe Ya'alon reported that Hamas had retained roughly 2,000 rockets and mortars from its arsenal of 10,000-plus projectiles.

Had Hamas accepted the proposal six weeks earlier there would be 2,192 Palestinians still alive; 65 Israeli soldiers would not have lost their lives; and seven Israel civilians, including the four-year-old boy, would still be alive. All the claims of having beaten Israel is just so much hot air and bluff. But that is how Arabs are, they live in a fantasy world that has little to do with reality (see Chapter 2 *The Arab Mind* in this writer's book *Philistine: The Great Deception*).

On July 31 Comedy Central's Stephen Colbert lampooned the Israel-Gaza media controversy. Colbert refers to the hundreds of dead body shots shown on behalf of the Palestinians, but only shots of Israeli prime minister Netanyahu on Israel's behalf. Colbert said that "Israel's Netanyahu could not compete against all the dead bodies, but that's how war works!" Colbert then exclaims, "We know that whoever has the most dead bodies wins!" Hamas must also view the war much the same way as Colbert does, only it is serious while Colbert was making fun of the absurdity.

As mentioned before, Dr. Richard Landes, the director of the Center of Millennial Studies at Boston University coined the phrase "Pallywood" to describe Palestinian obfuscation and unmitigated lying in reporting news events. Indeed, trying to follow Hamas's logic about winning is about the same as understanding a drowning man filling his pockets with stones in order to keep himself afloat. Gaza lies in ruins; there is a combatant death ratio of at least 14 – 1; and the civilian death ratio stands at 189 – 1. Apparently, Stephen Colbert was correct. Hamas has won because it "has the most dead bodies." It also has the most catastrophic destruction of its buildings since the founding of Hamas. Who can possibly argue with their claim of victory in light of all that?

Israel says little, but its very existence on the world stage bears witness to a divine claim, a claim that its God, the God of Abraham, Isaac and Jacob watches over the nation. The One who called Israel into existence also bears silent witness that Israel belongs to God. This provokes the world into an uproar against the Jewish state and its people—God's chosen people.

21

Counting bodies

THE HAMAS-RUN GAZA Ministry of Health claims that 2,192 Palestinians had died since July 8 when the fighting began, until this time of writing. It also claims that 84 percent of the Gazan death toll is civilian. Civilian casualties in Gaza are high due to Hamas ordering the population to remain in their homes during Israeli air-strikes; the civilian population in Gaza is used as a virtual human shield. There are no shelters for it to run to, and when civilians do take shelter in UN schools Hamas will fire rockets from the school in order to draw an Israeli response to the firing. The same holds true for hospitals and other sensitive places like cemeteries. The IDF counted and documented rocket firings between July 8 and August 15; there were 597 rockets fired from schools, cemeteries, mosques, churches, and hospitals.

Hamas has deliberately placed its rocket launchers in the middle of its civilian population and has fired more than 4,560 rockets into Israel during the past five weeks. This is an integral part of Hamas's war strategy. This strategy has been repeated each time its jihadist forces fire prolonged, massive rocket barrages into Israel—2008–2009, 2012, 2014. Civilian casualties result when Israel tries to destroy rockets and launchers from the air and this is turned into what the KGB called *"agitprop"*—the use of media for political agitation and propaganda. Israel's defensive actions are twisted by Hamas and they influence world media into changing the storyline—Gaza's population becomes the victim and Israel becomes the monster that purposely kills civilians.

When it comes to Gazan civilian casualty figures, without stopping to think about them they appear catastrophic; however, the figures are very deceptive. Casualty figures akin to Hamas's list above are also given by the UN Human Rights Council (UNHRC), the Al Mezan Center for Human Rights, and the Palestinian Center for Human Rights (PCHR). The numbers given are virtually the same, the only real difference lies in the percentages of civilian casualties—72 percent for the UNHRC, 82 percent for Al Mezan, and 84 percent for the PCHR, which is the same as Hamas.

Before we proceed further it should clearly understood by readers that when "human rights" enter into discussions relating to the Israel-Palestinian conflict, "human rights" is merely a euphemism for "Palestinian rights." From all accounts Israelis have no rights.

The UNHRC is daggers-drawn when it comes to Israel and it is by far the most anti-Israel office of the UN, which itself is the most anti-Semitic organization in the world. Al Mezan and the PCHR only mention Israel because it is the address for their hate-filled anti-Semitic barbs; they usually refer to Israel as "the zionist entity" or "the occupation."

The Hamas-run Gaza health ministry makes the claim that all Palestinian casualties are "innocent" and "martyrs," but makes no differentiation between the dead, apart from "men," "women," or "children."

IDF forces also faced suicide bombers in Gaza; and when the body parts were scrutinized by medics, two of the suicide bombers were definitively identified as female. So, who among the dead was a combatant and who was a non-combatant? The lines are blurred, all but invisible; both males and females took part in the fighting, and both would dress in civilian attire.

As it was pointed out earlier, some terrorist gunmen wore women's clothing, and two foreign journalists reported seeing men dressed in women's clothing with rifles poking out from under their gowns. A medical worker in Gaza quipped that a person needed to arrive at the Emergency Room with a weapon in hand before he could be classified as a combatant.

There were uniformed men and men dressed civilian clothing actively firing weapons, but Hamas also has many political figures, members of its security service and employees of its ministries. In Israeli eyes, anyone affiliated with the organization, which professes a goal of destroying Israel, is a combatant.

The IDF claimed that, based on field reports from active units, it had killed between 800 and 1,000 combatants. Israeli politicians, citing a study by an Israeli counter-terrorism group that is impressive in its documentation, say that between 47 and 50 percent of the Palestinian casualties were "fighters." Human rights groups have also acknowledged that people killed by Hamas as collaborators would be part of the count, and that people who died naturally, or perhaps through domestic violence, are likely counted as well. A 50 percent civilian death toll is, however, considered to be average in any war, thus the number of Gazan casualties were "normal"— excuse the somewhat callous use of that word.

The Meir Amit Intelligence and Terrorism Information Center, an Israeli group that analyzes terror and conflict deaths, accused the Hamas-controlled Health Ministry of "concealment and deception" in order "to create an ostensibly factual infrastructure for a political, propaganda, and legal campaign against Israel."

The political echelons in Israel have long held to the IDF argument that hundreds of young men among the casualties in the ongoing hostilities between Israel and Hamas were actual gunmen. Casualties cannot all be labeled civilians simply because they wear civvies. Apparently, some formerly hostile-to-Israel folk are now beginning to question the casualty figures coming from Gaza, the BBC and New York Times being in the forefront of those querying Gaza's "facts." Following is an analysis of the casualty count, the breakdown was done by the English-language Times of Israel, its analysis is practically identical to that provided by the UN Human Rights Council.

The Times of Israel analysis looks at 1,431 names and shows that the population most likely to be militants, men whose ages are 20 to 29, is also the most overrepresented in the death toll: They are nine percent of Gaza's 1.7 million residents, but 34 percent of those killed whose ages were provided for the analysis. At the same time, women and children under 15, the least likely to be legitimate targets, were the most underrepresented, making up 71 percent of the population and 33 percent of the known-age casualties.

Anthony Reuben, the BBC's head of statistics, cites figures published by the UN's High Commissioner for Human Rights, which found the number of civilian men killed in the fighting (725) outnumbered the number of women (214) by a factor of nearly 3.5 to 1. When the 216 confirmed "members of armed groups" are included, the disparity grows even larger. Reuben notes:

> If the Israeli attacks have been 'indiscriminate,' as the UN Human Rights Council says, it is hard to work out why they have killed so many more civilian men than women.

Aha! Reuben is beginning to see the logic behind UNHRC and Hamas statements which accuse Israel of deliberately targeting civilians. Had Israel targeted civilians the casualty rates for men and women would be reversed. The disparity between the sexes is due to Israel targeting gunmen and rocketeers and, unfortunately, civilians who have not heeded Israel's warnings to flee a particular building, also get killed when missiles and bombs explode.

Israel stands accused of destroying thousands of Palestinian homes. Israel readily admits that it targeted homes of Hamas commanders, which were being used as command centers, and also homes that were being used as weapons storage areas. Mosques and hospitals are also used as centers for gunmen and rocket storage; Israel targeted 41 mosques and one hospital, reducing them to ruins. The lower floors of the main Shifa hospital in Gaza is used as command centers by both Hamas and the Palestinian Islamic Jihad, whose leaders roam through the hospital's corridors. Foreign journalists have confirmed the presence of terrorists traipsing through the hospital, but no journalist or civilian was allowed onto the two lowest floors. Israel has thus far refrained from bombing the hospital due to the catastrophic death toll that would result from such a strike.

The hospital which the IAF destroyed had relatively few patients and plenty of advance warning to evacuate. Before exploding the building—with a number of gunmen still firing from its windows—the custodian informed the IDF by telephone that the building was empty and that the doors had been locked. Israel could not undertake the same procedure with the Shifa hospital because all the Hamas and Islamic Jihad commanders would flee the building—merged in with patients and medical personnel. In order to clear Shifa hospital of its terrorist command center presence there needs be a courageous Israeli commando raid which, according to the commander of the Gaza operation, would "pull them out by the ears."

What has not received any overseas publicity is the fact that Hamas deliberately exploded thousands of homes in Gaza itself, most likely in order to make it look worse for Israel on television screens around the world. It is almost unbelievable that a group would destroy its own people's homes and leave them destitute in order to cause Israel diplomatic pain. However, this is where the real war is being fought, in people's minds. Many Israelis, especially children, are physiologically traumatized after enduring years of rockets, now numbering in the tens of thousands, which continue to be fired into Israel from Gaza. Millions of people overseas, who were glued to their television watching the utter devastation of Gaza, are seething with anger at Israel and protest in the tens of thousands against Israel. Leaders of Western nations speak out of both sides of their mouths. Out of one side they say Israel has the right to defend its citizens against Gaza rocket fire, while out of the other side they condemn Israel for doing so. Hamas played its cards well.

22

Netanyahu's head is on the block (1)

THE CEASEFIRE THAT ISRAEL entered into with Hamas on August 26 has many Israelis fuming. Even though the IAF destroyed a large part of Gaza—the most destruction of any war with Hamas, and more than the combined destruction wrought in the two previous wars—the war ended with Hamas still able to fire a hundred or more rockets and mortars into Israel every day, the most being in the evening and night of August 20 when more than 160 rockets were fired into Israel. These "rockets" are not fireworks—they are usually four to six-feet-long (1.2 to 1.8 meters) lethal missiles that have up to 220 pounds (100 kilograms) of explosives in their warheads; every "rocket" has the potential to kill any number of people who happen to be near the impact zone. From a single "rocket" that struck a house in the city of Ashkelon, causing extensive damage, paramedics treated 40 people who were subsequently evacuated to Barzilai Medical Center in the city. Most of the injured suffered wounds from broken glass and from falling objects.

Of the actual 4,564 rockets fired into Israel during the war they were responsible for the killing of seven Israelis and the wounding of hundreds. Had it not been for the mandatory bomb shelters and safe rooms in modern Israeli homes, and the compulsory public bomb shelters in every city and town in Israel, the casualty rate would have been enormous.

However, it was the Iranian-supplied mortars that caused the most casualties. Mortars are only short range projectiles, but Hamas used them to devastating effect. Mortars accounted for more of the Israeli civilian deaths than did the rockets and they also took the lives of three soldiers. Mortars were fired into homes, schools, and kindergartens, and both the Kerem Shalom border crossing—through which truck loads of humanitarian aid was daily being delivered to Gaza during the war—and the Erez border crossing, which facilitates human and vehicle traffic to and from Gaza, especially for Gazans requiring medical aid or hospitalization. Both crossings were closed temporarily more than once due to damage from mortar attacks.

It was the residents of southern Israel that bore the brunt of the rockets and mortars. Fifty to 100 times or more each day the population had to dive for shelter when sirens sounded the warning of incoming rockets. In Tel Aviv and Jerusalem there were 90 seconds to find shelter before rockets would hit, but in the south of Israel the people only had 15 seconds to get to a bomb shelter. After living through Israel's longest war since 1948 and having to run for cover each few minutes many people are as mad as hornets at Prime Minister Binyamin Netanyahu for accepting a ceasefire. Most Israelis know full well that it is only a matter of time before an even worse time of war will hit them, and some Israelis are angry, especially those whose homes are in southern Israel—they are very angry indeed.

Hamas had been humiliatingly defeated. There is no other way of describing the ceasefire terms. It gained nothing from the ceasefire apart from a very restricted opening of the Rafah border crossing with Egypt. The crossing will be strictly supervised by the Egyptian security forces, and they are not about to let Hamas import weapons and explosives, or the raw materials to manufacture them.

Senior Hamas leaders will not be allowed to leave the Strip via the Rafah crossing due to Egypt recognizing Hamas as a terror organization being that it is an offshoot of the Egyptian Muslim Brotherhood with which Egypt is at war. Muhammed Morsi, former Egyptian president and former leader of the Muslim Brotherhood, is being held in prison on several charges that carry the death penalty. Also, several hundreds of Muslim Brotherhood leaders and activists have already been found guilty of crimes against the state; these are waiting for their death sentences to be carried out. Three *al-Jazeera* English journalists have also been found guilty of crimes against the Egyptian Republic and have been sentenced to lengthy prison terms. Indeed, Egypt will be keeping a very close eye on who and what goes across its border with Gaza.

Israel agreed to open its border crossings to allow humanitarian aid in, which is nothing new because truckloads of aid were being ferried into Gaza every day during the war. Palestinians requiring specialized medical treatment were moved to and fro through Israel's Erez crossing, so there is nothing new there either. Some reconstruction materials will be allowed into Gaza, but again, the crossing is under Israel's jurisdiction and its security services will only allow materials into Gaza for small reconstruction jobs, and once inside Gaza it will then be supervised by an international body to prevent Hamas using it for its own purposes.

On September 16 *Reuters* reported that the UN, Israel, and the PA had reached a "stop-gap" deal to allow reconstruction work to begin in the war-ravaged Gaza Strip. The UN will provide "security assurances" that its monitoring of the use of materials will prevent them for being used for non-civilian purposes such as Hamas command bunkers and cross-border attack tunnels. The agreement calls for the UN to ensure that the materials are "not diverted from their entirely civilian purpose."

Therefore, in reality, Hamas has been hamstrung. It has been dealt a deadly blow and will now be prevented from rebuilding its military infrastructure, albeit the UN monitors will likely run like rabbits once confronted by Hamas like other international monitors did before them.

That Hamas had been dealt a lethal blow was becoming increasingly obvious from its groveling after a longterm ceasefire. Israel's unrelenting and utterly devastating air-strikes—the IAF is reported to have only used ten percent of its airpower—reduced Hamas to begging for them to stop. Yet, once they stopped, the leaders crawled out from their rabbit holes below Shifa hospital and claimed victory.

That, however, was nothing new; it was entirely predictable. After every war the Arabs have had the gall to claim victory, even when massive armies had been decimated and virtually every shred of hardware—planes, armored personnel carriers, tanks, artillery pieces and so forth—had been obliterated. Arab armies claimed victory in Israel's 1948–49 War of Independence, albeit they continue to refer to that time as the Nakbar, the "Catastrophe." This writer mentioned in the last post that Arabs live in a fantasy world. It is a world completely foreign to Westerners; it is a world where if you can imagine something and somehow express it in words, it becomes fact.

Thus, in the wars with Israel, the Arabs by their own admission defeated Israel in 1948–49, 1956, 1967, 1973, 1982, 2006, 2008–2009, 2012, and most recently, in 2014.

Years ago a "Christian" Arab worker lit into this writer for being an Israeli and said, "Israel starts all the wars, we win them, and we still lose our land!" Not wanting to get into the same old ridiculous circle of arguments with him this writer simply said, "You're a Christian aren't you?," to which he replied, "Yes, I was raised in a Catholic school." This writer then said, "So, what did Jesus say about loving your enemies?" His reply gave an insight into the souls of "Christian" Arabs. He said, "Jesus says, 'Fight! Kill them all!'"

23

Netanyahu's head is on the block (2)

IN THE QU'RAN (KORAN), the Muslim holy book, there are 103 verses that instruct Muslims to fight and to kill for Allah, the god of Islam. The Qu'ran informs its Muslim adherents that they are to kill all infidels (non-Muslims) wherever they find them, especially the Jews who are, the Qu'ran asserts, the "sons of pigs and monkeys." If this writer has said it once, he has said it 500 times, "There is no peace, there will be no peace, and there can be no peace until Jesus returns to rule and reign from Jerusalem." It is just not going to happen all the while more than a billion Muslims are taught to hate and kill non-Muslims, especially the Jews whom their god Allah has cursed. There are verses in the Qu'ran that says that a believer (a Muslim) must "not kill another believer" and must not "kill any man without good cause." That, of course, is a license to kill, it leaves the door wide open for a Muslim to kill whomever he wants. Thus the Sunni Muslims are killing the Shia Muslims and vice versa throughout the Middle East because neither sect believes the other is a believer and should, therefore, be killed wherever they are found. Get the point? Others had said it before this writer did that "Not all Muslims are terrorists, but almost all terrorists are Muslims."

For over a decade before entering the new millennium this writer gave notice in meetings around the world, and also through a number of his books, that it had been written for three hundred years that the twenty-first century would be "the century of Islam," when all the world must bow to Islam. In those days this writer said that as we enter the new millennium Islamic terror would gather pace until it engulfs the world. We see this very thing happening before our eyes, and for the main part Western leaders are acting like politically correct zombies, always making excuses for Islam.

Hamas, the terror organization that controls the Gaza Strip, kept firing rockets until the last moment before the ceasefire. It proved a capacity for resilience to Israeli air-strikes even though it was the population of Gaza that paid the price for Hamas's resilience. We should bear in mind that neither the IDF nor the Israeli government sought at any point to bring Hamas down. Some members of the government, together with the majority of the Israeli public, wanted Hamas taken down, but that was not Prime Minister Binyamin Netanyahu's objective. He wanted to weaken Hamas by hitting it very hard, but he also wanted to ensure Hamas's capacity to survive—to enable it to continue to serve as the Gaza leadership address, a somewhat quasi partner to deal with. Defense Minister Moshe Ya'alon summed up Operation Protective Edge when he said that the IDF "navigated the operation according to our compass and not the weather vane that was heated from outside." Ya'alon's perspective of victory and his objective in the war was "to bring the other side to a ceasefire in accordance with your conditions." That objective was admirably accomplished.

With ISIS (Islamic State) on Israel's eastern border, Hamas on its southern border, and Hizb'allah on its northern border, toppling Hamas at that time could have opened the way for hell itself to come to Israel's shores.

Many Israelis are hot under the collar with Netanyahu for not toppling Hamas, but Netanyahu is not a fool, he is very pragmatic. Netanyahu was a captain in Israel's most elite commando unit— he understands war. Netanyahu's older brother, Yonathan, led the same unit—the *crème de la crème* of Israeli commando units—in the famous Entebbe raid named Operation Thunderbolt. The raid took place 2,500 miles (4,000 kilometers) from home and it freed 103 Jewish hostages who were being held by Idi Amin after a plane with 248 passengers was hijacked by Palestinian terrorists and flown to Entebbe airport—all the non-Jewish passengers were freed upon the plane's landing. Israel's daring raid captured the attention of the world and a movie was made and appropriately called Operation Thunderbolt.

There are numerous intangibles that we know nothing about, but which clearly affected Netanyahu's decision to accept the ceasefire. The IDF believed it had destroyed the threat from Hamas's attack tunnels; had killed up to 1,000 terrorists, including 40 top

Hamas commanders; it had destroyed thousands of rockets, rocket launchers, arms depots, and weapon manufacturing facilities; it had knocked out hundreds of terrorist command centers; and it had foiled a number of terrorist attacks on Israel from the land, from the sea, and from the air. When asked if Israel would "get a long term calm," Netanyahu said:

> I think it is too early to tell. But I can say that the blows to Hamas, and our ability to keep them from rearming by supervising the borders, increase the chances that this will be achieved. If there isn't quiet and Hamas again starts a 'drizzle' of rocket fire on any part of the country, we will respond harder than we have until now. We are prepared for all possibilities.

However, most Israelis oppose the ceasefire with Hamas; they are unhappy with the truce and feel less secure than before the Gaza operation. In one poll 59 percent of Israelis said they were dissatisfied with Netanyahu's performance. Another poll on *Channel 10* television found that 55% were satisfied with Netanyahu. The *Channel 10* poll indicated that a large portion of the dissatisfaction with Netanyahu came from him not going far enough in the war. Seventy-five percent said he should have toppled Hamas.

A majority of poll respondents said war would restart in under a year, and 37 percent predicted it would happen in less than six months. Yet another poll showed Israelis believing that the IDF emerged as the victor in Operation Protective Edge even though Israel as a nation did not. Sixty-one percent of respondents agreed with the statement that the IDF had won while Israel had lost. Respondents expressed frustration with the ceasefire that ended the operation with Hamas still in power in the Gaza Strip. Fifty-eight percent said the IDF should have been allowed to continue the operation in order to degrade the terrorist organization's military abilities and called the truce a mistake that wastes the achievements of the IDF. Current Israeli discontent could affect Netanyahu's chance of getting elected again. He won the war with Hamas, now he must win the war with the Israeli people—his head is on the chopping block.

There are Israelis on both sides of the divide—for and against the ceasefire. It is understandable that those who live in the Gaza periphery communities are concerned that Hamas, as has been its wont over the years, will only wait a few months or a few years at best, before renewing its quest to destroy Israel. Khaled Mashaal, Hamas's terror chief who lives in Qatar, the "Club Med for terrorists" threatened on August 28 to resume fighting if Hamas's demands are not met. He also said that "the ceasefire was a loss for Hamas" and that Gaza will never disarm its "sacred" weapons. Apparently, after only two days of calm we have returned once again to square one.

As an interesting aside, Israel's *Channel 2*'s Ehud Ya'ari reported on August 28 that the Hamas folk are also unhappy with the ceasefire. Amad Al-Almi, a senior Hamas official who represented Gaza in Egypt during the ceasefire negotiations with Israel, evidently returned to Gaza to less than satisfied friends and coworkers. His fellow terrorists attacked him with baseball bats and among numerous other injuries broke both his legs. The reason for the attack on Al-Almi is not known, however, it was only one day earlier that Khaled Mashaal had told the Hamas leadership that the ceasefire agreement was a loss for Hamas. Readers can now guess why Al-Almi, as the Hamas negotiator, got such a rousing welcome on his return from Cairo.

24

Goldstone II

THE UN HUMAN RIGHTS Council, a body dominated by dictators and the Organization of Islamic Cooperation, conspired together with Hamas against Israel with the Goldstone Report, an official UN investigation into Israel's conduct during Operation Cast Lead against Hamas in 2008–2009. The report castigated Israel and accused it of committing war crimes and crimes against humanity. The evidence collected by Judge Richard Goldstone came from Hamas, Islamic Jihad, and various Palestinian and left-of-left Israeli human rights NGOs (Non Governmental Organizations) and Israel was pilloried worldwide as a result. However, Goldstone later retracted some of his vilifying statements in an op-ed published by the *Washington Post* on April 1, 2011. The first paragraph of Goldstone's lengthy piece reads:

> We know a lot more today about what happened in the Gaza war of 2008–09 than we did when I chaired the fact-finding mission appointed by the U.N. Human Rights Council that produced what has come to be known as the Goldstone Report. If I had known then what I know now, the Goldstone Report would have been a different document.

Sure, the Goldstone Report would have been a different document had Goldstone not been so naive as to believe hate-filled Islamic fanatics and self-hating Israeli Jews, but the damage had been done and it can never be repaired. A UN investigation into Operation Protective Edge has already been ordered by Navi Pillay, the head of UNHRC; she leveled charges of war crimes against Israel after just the first few hours of Operation Protective Edge. Adolf Hitler would have found a great ally in Pillay; she is more hostile toward Israel than Iran's Muhammad Ahmadinejad. Since its inception in 2008 the UNHRC has adopted a total of 109 resolutions, of which 50 condemn Israel. Considering what is going on around the world the UNHRC record of condemnations of Israel is an indictment of the UN body and shows just how anti-Semitic the UNHRC truly is.

Pillay has named Judge William Schabas to lead the investigation into Israel's actions in the third round of the ongoing fight between Israel and Hamas. Schabas is well known for his anti-Israel statements and is particularly hostile toward Prime Minister Binyamin Netanyahu, of whom he said in 2012—when Ehud Olmert was prime minister—"Netanyahu is the one I would most like to see in the International Criminal Court (ICC)." What chance has Israel to a fair investigation with Schabas heading it? The outcome has been predetermined; the document lacks only signatures.

The absolute one sidedness of the Goldstone report has virtually all of Israel referring to the upcoming UNHRC kangaroo court trial of Israel as Goldstone II. With a long list of negative anti-Israel remarks already under his belt, Schabas is now within reach of realizing his cherished dream of putting Israeli leaders in the ICC dock on charges of war crimes and crimes against humanity. His January 2013 statement during a talk that his "favorite would be Netanyahu within the dock of the ICC" is alone sufficient for him to recuse himself. Schabas recently attempted to justify his statement by saying, "When I said my favorite was Netanyahu. I was echoing the Goldstone Report." Obviously, Schabas had acted as judge and jury at that time, and also again in 2010 when he said:

> Why are we going after the president of Sudan for Darfur and not the president of Israel for Gaza? Because of politics.

Schabas is on record for stating that Hamas is "a political party representing Palestinian aspirations for a state," and when pressed he would not say if he considers Hamas to be a terrorist organization. Schabas would only say—with the utmost hypocrisy—"It would be inappropriate for me to say if Hamas is a terrorist organization," stressing that the investigation into Israel's actions must be conducted "in as neutral a manner as possible." (!)

Israel's ambassador to the UN, Ron Prosor, said, "Forming an investigatory committee headed by Schabas is like inviting ISIS to organize religious tolerance week at the UN." The UNHRC has stated that it stands behind Schabas's appointment as head of the committee. Of course it does; UNHRC is the most anti-Semitic organ of the most anti-Semitic organization in the world.

On August 15 Senator Charles Schumer urged the UNHRC to remove William Schabas as head of the probe into the recent Gaza conflict, citing his past comments against Israel, which, the senator said, rules Schabas out as a fair judge of the war. Schumer added that if Schabas is not removed, the US should stop its funding of the UNHRC as well as any participation in it.

On September 4 UN Watch, a Geneva-based watchdog, filed a legal request demanding Schabas quit the UN Gaza inquiry due to his well-known anti-Israel bias. Schabas had previously accused Israel of disproportionality during the war with Hamas and that Schabas was sympathetic to Hamas which he termed "a political party" representing the Palestinian people's aspiration for statehood. The head of UN Watch, Hillel Neuer, said:

> You can't spend several years calling for the prosecution of someone, and then suddenly act as his judge. It's absurd.

In an interview with the Arab-language daily *Asharq al-Awsat* on September 9 Schabas said:

> This is an investigation that is necessary. I will not resign. I do not hate Israel. I will put my prior positions aside. I will be impartial.

After saying that his past comments will not bias the investigation, Schabas adds a really snide, anti-Israel comment:

> Even if Spiderman was heading the probe, they [the Israelis] would've attacked him. Our people will be on the ground very soon.

Adding his voice calling for Schabas to recuse himself, Canada's Foreign Minister John Baird came out against Schabas's appointment, calling the new inquiry a "sham."

Any responsible judge possessing integrity would recuse himself from the investigation, but apparently Schabas has no integrity. He has determinedly made up his mind to haul Israeli political and military leaders before the ICC. Despite many and varied calls for him to recuse himself from the Gaza inquiry he is hanging on as the probe's chief investigator like a baby clinging to its mother's nipples.

Professor Mordechai Kremnitzer, former Dean of the Law Faculty at the Hebrew University of Jerusalem, says that by breaching its responsibility to be impartial, the UN Human Rights Council and its commission investigating alleged Israeli war crimes in Gaza are betraying international law.

Initial statements by the UNHRC indicate that it likely will accuse or imply accusations of war crimes against Israeli soldiers who fought in Gaza. The UNHRC also passed a resolution strongly condemning:

> [T]he widespread, systematic and gross violations of international human rights and fundamental freedoms arising from the Israeli military operations carried out in the Occupied Palestinian Territory, including that may amount to international crimes, directly resulting in the killing of Palestinians and the wanton destruction of homes, vital infrastructure and public properties.

This resolution essentially pre-determines Israel's guilt on all counts. The resolution's dates and areas are important: East Jerusalem since June 13, 2014. Why choose that date? Because it was the day the 16-year-old Palestinian boy Muhammed Abu Khdeir was murdered. The investigation could not begin the previous day because that was the day the Israeli teenagers, Gilad Sha'ar, aged 16, Naftali Fraenkel, also aged 16, and Eyal Yifrach, aged 19 years, were abducted and killed; and then the UNHRC would have to deal with the issue, but the boys were Israelis and Israelis have no value in the eyes of the UNHRC.

A glaring omission in the resolution—one that stands out like a sore thumb—is the lack of mentioning Hamas firing thousands of lethal missiles into Israeli population centers. But then, according to Schabas, Hamas is "a political party representing Palestinian aspirations for a state," therefore, in Schabas's eyes, Hamas was apparently acting legitimately when it launched 4,564 rockets and mortars into Israel with the express purpose of killing as many Israelis as possible. Obviously, the UNHRC deems the random firing of missiles on Israel's civilian population from power plants, public buildings, and civilian concentrations—thereby using women and children as human shields—as being consistent with international human rights and a people's fundamental freedoms.

The UN probe also excludes any investigation into the use of UN facilities in Gaza that were used to support Hamas in the war. Neither does it address the aiding and abetting of UNRWA officials in Hamas's terror activities. All told, three UN schools were found to have been used to store munitions; one of which was booby-trapped and took the lives of three Israeli soldiers; that could not have happened without the knowledge of senior UN officials. Another fact to be digested is that 25 of the 27 members of the UNRWA executive in Gaza are Hamas operatives—but why let facts get in the way of hurting Israel? Israel cannot expect justice from such a supposed august body as the United Nations because the UN is incapable of delivering justice whenever the Jewish state is in its cross-hairs. The UN is a toothless tiger in every arena apart from that of its hatred of Israel; its troops have run from battle in conflicts all around the world. The UN should concentrate on just being a humanitarian aid organization and leave conflicts to those who know which end of a gun the bullet comes from.

Israel refused to cooperate with the UN investigation into the 21-day 2008–2009 Operation Cast Lead, which spawned the UN's Goldstone Report. At the time of writing Jerusalem had not indicated whether it will or will not cooperate with the new UN probe of the 50-day Operation Protective Edge, already dubbed Goldstone II. Richard Goldstone had the humility to publicly retract some of the harsh criticisms of Israel that were presented in the Goldstone Report; however, no one in Israel will be holding their breath in hope for similar humility to emanate from William Schabas.

Dore Gold, a former Israeli ambassador to the UN; now an adviser to Prime Minister Netanyahu, said:

> You can't go into any kind of legal proceeding when the judge and jury have decided you are guilty before you have even walked into the courtroom.

Gold says he opposes cooperating with the panel. He wants Israel to refuse to be part of what he calls "a circus."

Israel is becoming more and more isolated as NGOs and labor unions—predominantly British—institute academic, cultural, and goods boycotts across the Western world. Israel's destiny is to stand alone with its God, *the Holy One of Israel* (Psalms 78:41 and many other places) and that day is fast approaching. Few and far between are Israel's friends. The present occupant of the White House has shown himself to be no friend of Israel; however, Israel has many friends within the United States Congress and there would be a revolt in Congress if Obama were to touch Israel and put his finger in the eye of the Almighty (Zechariah 2:8).

On September 19, 2014, over three-quarters of the members of the Senate adopted bi-partisan legislation—the United States-Israel Strategic Partnership Act—that declared Israel to be a "major strategic partner" and which opened the way for increased cooperation in defense, energy, agriculture, and a number of other areas. The US will also increase its stockpile of weapons in Israel, which Israel could use in an emergency, providing the weapons stockpiles were immediately replenished by Israel. The bill reaffirms and broadens the US-Israel alliance during this most critical time in the Middle East.

If push comes to shove in the UN Security Council over William Schabas's Goldstone II report, the recognition that Israel is a "major strategic partner" all but guarantees a US veto against hostile UN acts against Israel.

25

The fallout from premeditated barbarianism

IT IS UNFORTUNATELY TRUE that some people have to be taught that evil doing has inevitable consequences. Some people have to be literally shocked out of continuing their evil ways; Israel recently shocked Hamas like it had never been shocked before.

When this writer began his blog posts titled "The Fallout From Premeditated Barbarism," there was no war. This writer had a point that he wished to make at the time; that point is even more pertinent now that the dust of Operation Protective Edge is beginning to settle.

Everything concerning Operation Protective Edge began with the premeditated abduction and murders of three innocent Israeli teenagers. In an overt display of premeditation the terrorists procured a car specifically for the abduction and attempted to destroy the evidence of the murders by torching the car.

Some Israelis called for revenge, and three of them abducted and murdered an innocent Palestinian teenager—murdering him in a most brutal and obscene way. That the act was also premeditated is borne out by the fact that they had earlier attempted to abduct a nine-year-old Palestinian girl.

Israeli Arabs called for revenge for the murder of the Arab teenager and took to violent demonstrations on the streets of Jerusalem, which gravitated to other Arab Israel towns. At this time of writing some 900 Arabs have been arrested for violent acts against Jews—stone-throwing at Israeli cars, buses, and Jerusalem's light railcars; firebombing Jewish homes and a gas (petrol) station with Molotov cocktails; throwing pipe-bombs, rocks, firecrackers, and Molotov cocktails at Israeli police trying to quell the unrest. Hundreds of injured have been treated by medics and hospitals, and two Arabs have lost their lives in the riots.

In sympathy with the murdered Arab teenager, Hamas began firing small salvos of rockets into Israel which prompted the IAF to respond with precision air-strikes against Hamas military targets. Hamas then upped its rocket fire, which brought a very heavy response from the IAF. Thus, in retaliation to IAF attacks upon its military and civil institutions, Hamas began terrorist infiltrations into Israel in attempts to kill or kidnap Israelis. The infiltrations spawned Israel's ground offensive that consequently wreaked havoc in Gaza and caused catastrophic damage. This writer's point is this: At this time of writing, since those three teenagers were kidnapped, some 2,267 people have lost their lives as a direct consequence of that abduction and murder. Tens of thousands of Palestinians, and a few thousand Israelis, are wounded; hundreds upon hundreds of Palestinians are crippled for life, along with scores of Israeli soldiers; and billions of dollars in damage has been wrought upon both Israeli, but predominantly Palestinian, homes and lifestyles. And we needs must remember the number of people, first and foremost children, who will be traumatized for the rest of their lives. This, then, is the fallout from premeditated barbarianism. And it could all so easily have been avoided; it was hatred of Jews—which has its roots in the teachings of the Qu'ran— that ignited this latest fireball between Israel and the Palestinians.

Hamas had originally denied carrying out the abductions of the Israeli teenagers, but said it applauded those who did. From the get-go Israel said it had proof Hamas had carried out the abductions and murders. During its ground offensive the IDF captured the Hamas operative who masterminded the abduction as he tried to flee to Jordan. Under interrogation the command-level operative revealed that the orders and financing for the abduction had indeed come from the Hamas leadership in Gaza. On September 4, 2014, Hussam Hassan Kawasme, the Hamas mastermind of the kidnapping-murder of the three Israeli teenagers in June, was indicted in an Israeli Military Court.

Breaking news came on September 23, 2014: the two terrorists, Marwan Kawasme—brother of the above indicted mastermind—and Amer Abu Aysha, who both carried out the abduction and murders of the Israeli teens were killed in a firefight with Israeli troops during a capture attempt following a long manhunt that had been ongoing since June 13. The operation was carried out by the Shin Bet along with IDF soldiers and troops from an anti-terror police unit. IDF troops had narrowly missed finding the two wanted terrorists on several occasions and security forces had received fresh information on the whereabouts of the two men from Hamas members arrested earlier. Both terrorists were killed after refusing to surrender and opening fire on Israeli troops surrounding their hiding place. "We opened fire, they returned fire and they were killed in the exchange," IDF spokesman Lieutenant-Colonel Peter Lerner told *Reuters*.

IDF Chief of Staff Lieutenant-General Benny Gantz thanked the security forces after the killing of the two Palestinian terrorists who had kidnapped and murdered the Israeli teens. Addressing Israel, Gantz said:

> On the eve of Rosh Hashanah, Operation Brother's Keeper, which began on June 13, 2014, and has been continued with determination this entire time, has come to an end. We promised the Sha'er, Yifrah, and Fraenkel families that we would find the murderers of their sons and we did.

Israeli media reported Hamas's confirmation of the deaths of the two terrorists. Hamas spokesman Hussam Badran said in a statement:

> Two members of the Izz A-Din al-Qassam Martyrs Brigades [Hamas's military wing], Marwan Kawasme and Amer Abu Aysha were killed after a journey of sacrifice and giving. This is the path of resistance and we walk it side by side.

At a Muslim scholar's conference in Turkey a Hamas official, Sheik Saleh al-Arouri, took credit for Hamas for the kidnapping and murder of the Israeli teenagers. Al-Arouri said, "I praise the brave action that the al-Qassam Brigades carried out."

The terrorists' kidnapping and killing of three teenagers was a "journey of sacrifice and giving"? It was a "brave action"? Who is kidding whom? Apparently, Islamic barbarianism has no limits.

The August 26 ceasefire called for renewed talks within one month to thrash out a longterm ceasefire. However, Hamas's kingpin, Khaled Mashaal, said in a speech he made in Qatar on September 13 that negotiating with Israel without "resistance" was like asking for charity. Mashaal said, "negotiations without a show of force and without resistance would be like begging for charity at the enemy's feet." His remarks prompted Israeli officials to question whether Hamas was really interested in renewing ceasefire negotiations with Israel; they evaluated Mashaal's remarks and assessed that the likelihood talks would resume was slim. Mashaal also said in his speech, "[The war in] Gaza taught us an important lesson, and that is that the enemy understands only the language of force."

As mentioned earlier, we are apparently back to square one. The talks in Cairo did resume, but due to the Jewish High Holidays they were soon postponed and slated to restart in the last week of October. Meanwhile, Hamas continues to rattle its sabers and declare that it controls the peace in southern Israel, not Netanyahu.

Saeb Erekat, Abu Mazen's chief negotiator, claimed on September 29 that Israel committed genocide when it killed "12,000 Palestinians" during Operation Protective Edge, of which "96 percent were civilians." This writer has repeatedly tried to make the point clear that Arabs live in a fantasy world in which reality and truth does not exist. However, Erekat's outrageous claim will be believed by many who greedily gobble up the continuous stream of fairy tales that come forth from the anti-Israel camp. Unfortunately, when mud is thrown, some of it will stick.

Israelis are already marking off their calendars. They are waiting for the next round of the seemingly never-ending war with Hamas to begin. However, there is a growing fear among Western nations that their own home-grown jihadists will return all fired-up from the conflicts in Syria and Iraq and begin committing standard jihadi atrocities at home.

Several jihadists have already returned home and have committed heinous murders in England, France, Belgium, and Israel, but those murders are merely the tip of an Islamic iceberg. There are thousands upon thousands of Western-raised jihadists fighting in Syria and Iraq. When most return home, become bored with the ubiquitous quiet of Western civilization, and start butchering and beheading Westerners, the international community of nations might, just might, understand Israel's actions against Hamas a little better. Hamas is a branch of the same tree as ISIS (Islamic State).

Some Western politicians may learn to hold their tongues a little when Islam rises up within their own nations; they may even learn to think twice before spitting out their heretofore knee-jerk condemnations of the Jewish state. Make no mistake, the Islamic jihadi chickens are coming home to roost in their Western host-nations.

For Your Information

Ramon Bennett, the author of this book, also writes the **Update**, the regular newsletter of the *Arm of Salvation Ministries*. The **Update** keeps readers informed on worldwide events that affect Israel, and also, on the ministry of Ramon Bennett and his wife, Zipporah. An annual donation of $20.00 is requested for the **Update** to offset production and first class postage costs. The **Update** is also available in PDF format at $15.00 per year, which subscribers receive weeks ahead of the mailed edition.

Subscription amounts for the PDF **Update** and additional donations should be made to Ramon Bennett and sent to the address below. Alternatively, readers can subscribe online at: http://www. ShekinahBooks.com.

Arm of Salvation (AOS) was founded by Ramon Bennett in 1980 and is an indigenous Israeli ministry dependent upon gifts and the proceeds from its book and music sales to sustain its work in and for Israel and the Jewish people.

Copies of **GAZA!** and other books by Ramon Bennett (see following pages), together with albums of popular Hebrew worship songs composed by Zipporah Bennett, are available from:

Shekinah Books LLC
755 Engleby Drive
Colorado Springs, CO 80930 U.S.A.
Telephone (719) 645-7722
eMail: usa@ShekinahBooks.com.

All payments must be in U.S. funds drawn on a U.S. bank. Feel free to visit our website: http://www. ShekinahBooks.com to purchase, subscribe, and/or donate via PayPal.

New from Shekinah!

Ramon Bennett's long-awaited autobiographical testimony book
— paperback 448 pages, or e-book

This is a book that some have waited years to lay their hands upon. It is the extraordinary life story of a man who has been introduced as "someone who has suffered the trials of Job."

All My Tears is the astounding story of an unwanted, abused child whom God adopted and anointed, and is using for His glory.

Often verging on the unbelievable; the author in his youth suffered physical and sexual abuse. In adult life he survived national economic meltdown; ultra high-speed car crashes; boat capsizes; several "incurable" diseases; and a head-first dive into a concrete post in a horse riding accident that broke his cheekbones and left him with headaches from a broken neck that was only discovered during a spinal operation 37 years later.

This is the story of a man's love for God, and of God's obvious love for the man; the two continue to walk and work together five decades after their first encounter. And miracles keep happening.

    To purchase the above book go to:
http://www.shekinahbooks.com

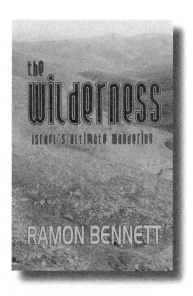

"*VERY INFORMATIVE BOOK FOR THOSE WHO are looking for answers to what is happening in the middle east. Most of what you hear in the news media is such surface stuff and news to steer you away from the truth. God's Word is truth and Ramon Bennett breaks down verses that I've wondered about for years. A very good read, you won't be able to put it down.*"

– William D. Douglas

335 pages – Paperback or e-book

For a descriptive overview of the above book, or to purchase go to:
http://www.shekinahbooks.com

"*WHEN DAY & NIGHT CEASE is the most comprehensive, factual and informative book on Israel—past, present and future I have ever read... If you want a true picture of how Israel is falling into Bible prophecy today, look no further. You will want to read this book.*"

         – Freda Lindsay *Christ For the Nations, Inc.*

"*...the best book I have read in 10 years...*"

         – Book reviewer, *Christianity Today, U.K.*

306 Pages – Paperback

For a descriptive overview of the above book, or to purchase go to:

http://www.shekinahbooks.com

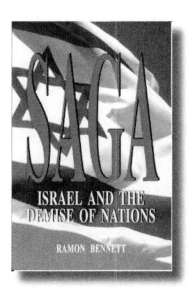

UNDERSTAND the chaos taking place around the world today! SAGA is about Israel and Israel's God; about war and judgment—past, present, and future. Nations came and went, empires rose and fell; and God is still judging nations today. A "must read" in light of world events today.

I spent the weekend with Saga—Wow!   – Pat Caulfield, The Ryan Law Office.

237 Pages – Paperback

For a descriptive overview of the above book, or to purchase go to:
http://www.shekinahbooks.com

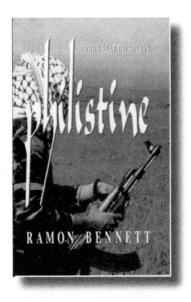

PHILISTINE lays bare the Arab mind, Islam, the United Nations, the media, rewritten history and the Israeli-PLO peace accord. *PHILISTINE* will grip you. *PHILISTINE* will inform you. *PHILISTINE* will shock you. Until you read *PHILISTINE* you will never understand the Middle East—the world's most volatile region.

"The whole world needs to read PHILISTINE" – Donna Fischer
"We wish we had more books like PHILISTINE" – Jerusalem Post Book Club

345 Pages – Paperback

SHEKINAH

For a descriptive overview of the above book, or to purchase go to:
http://www.shekinahbooks.com

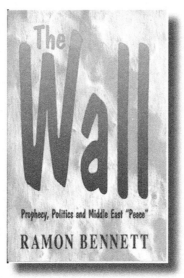

*"**THEY** lead My people astray, saying 'Peace!' when there is no peace, and because, when a flimsy wall is built, they cover it with whitewash"* (Ezekiel 13:10). Ramon Bennett exsposes the peace process for what it is, an attempt to break Israel down piece by piece:

"A truly prophetic book in the biblical sense ... Its impact is heavier than any other book [Bennett has] written."   – P.M. Switzerland

"... a powerful explosion of a book..."   – L.S. Norway

"...more than excellent!! ... brilliant..."   – M.F. Singapore

367 Pages – Paperback

SHEKINAH

For a descriptive overview of the above book, or to purchase go to:
http://www.shekinahbooks.com

Read how, a God-hungry Orthodox Jewish girl, found the Reality she longed for. This book, often amusing, will help readers understand the way Jewish people think and feel about the "Christian" Jesus.

137 Pages – Paperback – ISBN 965-90000-9-X

SHEKINAH

For a descriptive overview of the above book, or to purchase go to:
http://www.shekinahbooks.com

Kuma Adonai
"Arise O Lord!" – Songs of warfare and worship

Hebrew texts, translation, and transliterations printed inside the jacket

Hallelu
"Hallelu" – Dual Hebrew–English songs of worship

Hebrew texts, translation, and transliterations printed inside the jacket

Mi Ha'amin?
"Who Hath Believed?" – Hebrew and Aramaic prophecies in song

Hebrew texts, translation, and transliterations printed inside the jacket

SHEKINAH

For a descriptive overview of the above albums, or to purchase go to:

http://www.shekinahbooks.com

Printed in Great Britain
by Amazon

24647565R00086